THE LONDON OF
CHARLES DICKENS

The London of Charles Dickens

Foreword by Monica Dickens
Designed and illustrated by
Peter Roberson

LONDON TRANSPORT and MIDAS BOOKS

© LONDON TRANSPORT EXECUTIVE 1970, 1979

First published in 1970 to
mark Dickens Centenary

Published in 1979 by Midas Books
12 Dene Way
Speldhurst, Kent TN3 0NX
in association with London Transport

ISBN 0 85936 197 7 (Cased)
ISBN 0 85936 230 2 (Limp)

Printed in Great Britain by Billing & Sons Ltd.
Guildford, London and Worcester

Foreword

SAM WELLER's knowledge of London was said to be 'extensive and peculiar'. With even greater truth this could have been said of my great-grandfather. He could name a certain table in a certain inn, where one leg was missing, to the greater convenience of the customer imbibing his brandy and water, warm; a little pub where coal-heavers danced by the river; a staymaker's in Belgravia, where on the ground floor, a life-size model in a blue petticoat, stay-lace in hand, looked over her shoulder at the town in innocent surprise to find herself dressing in such circumstances. He knew a street in Bethnal Green where a party of fowls, the lord of the family with a paucity of feathers and the lady with the appearance of a bunch of office pens, pecked at kettles and saucepans; neighbourhoods where the majority of inhabitants devoted themselves to the healthful and invigorating pursuit of mangling; streets where swivel bridges let in roaming monsters of ships among the houses. He could take you to churches with their own particular flavours of wine or tea or spice or damaged oranges or herrings, and hassocks stuffed with the produce of the neighbourhood. He knew where there were houses like bottles filled with a strong distillation of mews.

We call it The London of Charles Dickens. Thousands of visitors to this country make pilgrimages to these odd little relics of a man's imaginative vision. Many have disappeared, some in wartime, some fallen under the pick and bulldozer of the speculative builder. Quaint little corners in the City have been swallowed up and covered over by great, square, characterless blocks of concrete and glass and so the places that are left, and the sites of those that have gone, are all the more precious and worth recording. Hence this little volume – *The London of Charles Dickens*.

London is changing – inevitably – but it is to be hoped that those who plan its future will manage to preserve some of these old places, to remind us that not everything in Dickens's time was dark and ugly. As G. K. Chesterton wrote about Mr Pickwick – . . . *he is the abstract wanderer and wonderer, the Ulysses of comedy; the half-human and half-elfin creature – human enough to wander, human enough to wonder, but still sustained with that merry fatalism that is natural to immortal beings – sustained by that hint of divinity which tells him in the darkest hour that he is doomed to live happily ever afterwards. He has set out walking to the end of the world, but he knows he will find an Inn there.* Let us hope the planners will leave him and his companions some odd corners in Dickens's London to rest their immortal shades.

Why are these literary associations so important? Because with Dickens, fiction becomes stronger than fact. In the Dickens House at 48 Doughty Street, now preserved by the Dickens Fellowship as a Museum, where the novelist lived as a young man, long-haired and flamboyant, and where he became famous, are two windows. One is a small window from an attic of a house in Bayham Street, Camden Town, where Dickens lived as a boy when his father was in the Marshalsea Debtors' Prison. The other is an equally small larder window, from a house in Chertsey. We are 'assured' that it was the window through which Bill Sikes put Oliver Twist on the occasion of the burglary. That little window of the imaginary small boy seems just as important as the one through which the living lonely little boy gazed out on to his world.

We lunch at the George and Vulture Inn, off Cornhill, not only because it is very old, not only because Dickens lunched there, but because Mr Pickwick, when asked by Bob Sawyer where he *hung out*, replied that he was at present *suspended at the George and Vulture.*

We can wander through the Inns of Court and find delightful nooks and corners of that past age, still used by the lawyers of today. On the door posts we can still see long lists of names of 'gentlemen of the long robe', who occupy these chambers.

We can walk in Lincoln's Inn Fields where, said Dickens, in large houses *lawyers lie like maggots in nuts*, or walk into Staple Inn, *the turning into which out of the clashing street imparts to the relieved pedestrian the sensation of having put cotton in his ears and velvet soles on his boots.* We can still get that sensation today, just as Dickens did. In places like these, his London is still ours, and very much alive.

A walk through these Inns of Court discovers peace and pleasure in the kindly surroundings of warm red brick, and bright green grass and ancient trees. When imagination peoples these courtyards with the immortal characters of Dickens, his whole world becomes fascinatingly alive.

In Middle Temple, we can see again the rough Hugh visiting his patron, the elegant Sir John Chester (BARNABY RUDGE). In Fountain Court, with its *plash of falling water*, John Westlock meets Ruth Pinch (MARTIN CHUZZLEWIT). In Garden Court, the convict Magwitch, back from Australia, reveals himself to Pip as the unsuspected source of his *great expectations*. In Pump Court walks the gentle Tom Pinch and his mysterious employer, old Martin Chuzzlewit. Along King's Bench Walk, we can imagine the figure of Sydney Carton sobering himself before turning into Stryver's chambers in Paper Buildings (A TALE OF TWO CITIES). At Whitefriars Gate, Pip receives the sinister message from Wemmick – *Don't go Home* (GREAT EXPECTATIONS), and Rogue Riderhood slouches past Temple Church on his way to Mortimer Lightwood's office, and Mr Dolls, well loaded with threepennorth's of rum, staggers to the same destination (OUR MUTUAL FRIEND).

All the Inns of Court can be peopled like this, away from the noise and smell of cars and traffic jams. In this little book are notes to remind the visitor to London of these many associations, in the hope that they will add interest to the visit and make it something to be remembered.

This is Dickens's London – the London in which he lived and suffered and triumphed – the London of his books. Touch it with his imaginative wand, and its streets will once more resound to the clatter of horses' hooves and the cries of old London. It will once again become the teeming background to the fascinating stories of this famous Englishman, who lies in a peaceful corner of Westminster Abbey, where people still gather to give silent thanks to him for the books that he has left us.

Monica Dickens.

Publisher's Note

London Transport gratefully acknowledges the help of the Dickens Fellowship, its Hon. Secretary, Mr. John Greaves, A.C.I.S., and Mrs. Gwen Major, who have made themselves responsible for the vast task of compiling, sifting, selecting and finally checking all the Dickens references in the text. Without their expert and scholarly assistance this contribution to the Dickens Centenary celebrations would have been impossible.

The Dickens Fellowship wishes particularly to thank for their valuable help Mr. Mostyn Harper of the Fellowship, and also Miss Jean Ward, who typed the text for Mr. Cedric C. Dickens (Past-President of the Dickens Fellowship).

Throughout the book extracts from Dickens's own writings are shown in italics. LIFE refers to the LIFE OF CHARLES DICKENS, a contemporary biography by John Forster.

Adelphi Arches (demolished) *I was fond of wandering about the Adelphi because it was a mysterious place with those dark arches. I see myself emerging one evening from some of these arches on a little public house,* (Fox-under-the-Hill, now demolished) *close to the river . . . some coal heavers were dancing. . . .* DAVID COPPERFIELD CH. XI; LIFE

Later, on the advice of his aunt, Betsey Trotwood, David took lodgings in the Adelphi and remembered his poverty-stricken boyhood when he would wander down the arches. These and other experiences of the boy David were obviously memories of Charles Dickens's own childhood. DAVID COPPERFIELD CH. XXIII

Adelphi Hotel, now demolished, at the corner of Adam Street, named 'Osborne's' in PICKWICK PAPERS, was Mr. Wardle's favourite stopping place when in London. Mr. Pickwick came here for a celebration after his release from the Fleet Prison, and it was in this Hotel that the fat boy stuck a fork into Mr. Pickwick's leg to draw his attention. PICKWICK PAPERS CH. LIV

Adelphi Terrace Following Tattycorum and Rigaud to this Terrace, Arthur Clennam saw them meet Miss Wade and witnessed the scene that followed. LITTLE DORRIT BOOK ii, CH. IX

Along here Mrs. Edson hurried, fortunately to be saved by Mrs. Lirriper from an unhappy end. CHRISTMAS STORIES: MRS. LIRRIPER'S LODGINGS

Adelphi Theatre (rebuilt). Of the several grades of lawyer's clerks, *There is the salaried clerk . . . who devotes the major part of his thirty shillings a week to his personal pleasure and adornment* (and) *repairs half-price to the Adelphi Theatre at least three times a week.* PICKWICK PAPERS CH. XXXI

Ailsa Park Villas, St. Margarets, Twickenham. At No. 4, now Down House, Charles Dickens lived for some part of 1838. LIFE

Albany, Piccadilly. *He lived in chambers in the Albany, did Fledgeby, and maintained a spruce appearance.* OUR MUTUAL FRIEND BOOK ii, CH. V; BOOK iii, CH. I; BOOK iv, CH. VIII

Aldersgate Street Arthur Clennam, having parted from Doyce, walked down this way to St. Paul's where he found John Baptist, knocked down by a coach, on his way to St. Bartholomew's Hospital. LITTLE DORRIT BOOK i, CH. XIII

In a *hybrid hotel in a little square behind Aldersgate Street* John Jasper stayed when in London – said to have been Falcon Hotel, once in Falcon Square on the right. EDWIN DROOD CH. XXIII

The Lively Turtle went to *Mrs. Skim's Private Hotel and Commercial Lodging House, near Aldersgate Street, City. . . .* This could also have been the Falcon Hotel. MISCELLANEOUS PAPERS: THE LIVELY TURTLE

The Albion Hotel, now gone, stood nearly opposite the entrance from Aldersgate Street to Bartholomew's Close. Here Dickens entertained his friends in 1839 to celebrate the completion of NICHOLAS NICKLEBY. LIFE

Aldgate *Mr. Blotton (of Aldgate)* . . . was a worthy inhabitant of this part; exactly where is unknown! PICKWICK PAPERS CH. I

Aldgate Avenue, site of the Bull Inn, from which Mr. Pickwick started for Ipswich in a coach driven by Mr. Tony Weller. PICKWICK PAPERS CH. XX, XXII

At a meeting in certain Barbican cellars of the secret Society of 'Prentice Knights, a novice, one *Mark Gilbert, age nineteen, bound to Thomas Curzon, hosier, Golden Fleece, Aldgate,* was installed a member. BARNABY RUDGE CH. VIII

David arrived at the Blue Boar (near to the Bull) from Blunderstone, en route for Salem House. *I forget,* he says, *whether it was the 'Blue Bull' or the 'Blue Boar'; but I know it was the Blue something, and that its likeness was painted up on the back of the coach.* The effigy of the Blue Boar was retained by the tobacco factory at No. 31 Aldgate High Street (now demolished). DAVID COPPERFIELD CH. V

Aldgate Pump At the junction of Fenchurch and Leadenhall Streets. After the return of Walter Gay, when Mr. Toots could not bear to see the happiness of Florence with him – so unlike unselfish Mr. Toots – he left *the little company that evening . . . to take a little turn to Aldgate Pump and back.* DOMBEY AND SON CH. LVI

The old gentleman over the garden wall to Mrs. Nickleby: *. . . or is it in consequence of the statue at Charing Cross having been lately seen on the Stock Exchange at midnight, walking arm-in-arm with the Pump from Aldgate, in a riding habit?* NICHOLAS NICKLEBY CH. XLI

On his way to see over the Wapping Workhouse, Dickens noted the Aldgate Pump as he passed it. UNCOMMERCIAL TRAVELLER: WAPPING WORKHOUSE

Shabby gentility . . . is as purely local as the statue at Charing Cross or the pump at Aldgate. SKETCHES BY BOZ: SHABBY GENTEEL PEOPLE

All Souls' Church, Langham Place. The picture on which Sam Weller's eyes were fixed depicted *a couple of human hearts, skewered together with an arrow . . . a male and female cannibal in modern attire . . . a decidedly indelicate young gentleman, in a pair of wings and nothing else . . . a representation of the spire of the church in Langham Place, London, appeared in the distance . . . the whole formed a 'valentine'. . . .* PICKWICK PAPERS CH. XXXIII

'All the Year Round' Offices At No. 26 (formerly 11) Wellington Street, at the corner of Tavistock Street, was the office of ALL THE YEAR ROUND. The building still stands. Here Dickens furnished bachelor chambers in his later years, for use during his London reading season. LIFE

Angel, Islington . . . *it was nearly eleven o'clock when they* (Oliver and the Dodger) *reached the turnpike at Islington. They crossed from the Angel into St. John's Road.* OLIVER TWIST CH. VIII

Mr. Brownlow lived in Pentonville at the time he rescued Oliver from Fagin and Mr. Fang, the Hatton Garden magistrate. *The coach rattled away . . . and turning when it reached the Angel at Islington, stopped at length before a neat house in a quiet shady street near Pentonville.* OLIVER TWIST CH. XII

Aldgate Pump

Later, another two concerned with Oliver, Noah Claypole and Charlotte, arriving at the Angel, he *wisely judged from the crowd of passengers and number of vehicles, that London began in earnest.* OLIVER TWIST CH. XLII

Angel Place (or Court). See Borough.

Arundel Street (now largely rebuilt) No. 2 is the site of Chapman & Hall's publishing house, numbered then 187 Strand, where Dickens purchased the magazine containing his first effort at fiction *in all the glory of print.* LIFE

Astley's (Westminster Bridge Road, now demolished). *Dear, dear, what a place it looked that Astley's; with all the paint, gilding and looking-glass; the vague smell of horses suggestive of coming wonders. . . .* OLD CURIOSITY SHOP CH. XXXIX

Trooper George, paying a visit to Astley's, *is much delighted with the horses and feats of strength; looks at the weapons with a critical eye; disapproves of the combats, as giving evidences of unskilful swordsmanship; but is touched home by the sentiments.* BLEAK HOUSE CH. XXI

We like to watch a regular Astley's party in the Easter or mid-summer holidays – pa and ma, and nine or ten children, varying from five foot six to two foot eleven. SKETCHES BY BOZ: ASTLEY'S

Mr. Booley remarked that into whatever regions he extended his travels, and however wide the range of his experience became, he still found, on repairing to Astley's Amphitheatre, that he had much to learn. MISCELLANEOUS PAPERS: MR. BOOLEY'S VIEW OF THE LORD MAYOR'S SHOW

There was Horatio, sure enough, on a large black horse curvetting and prancing along like an Astley's supernumerary. SKETCHES BY BOZ: HORATIO SPARKINS

Athenaeum Club (Waterloo Place). Dickens was elected to this club in 1838. The lobby is memorable as the scene of the reconciliation between Dickens and Thackeray a few days before the latter's death. Meeting by accident in the lobby after a period of strained relationship, 'the unrestrained impulse of both was to hold out the hand of forgiveness and fellowship!' LIFE

The Athenaeum, Waterloo Place

Austin Friars Tom Pinch, on reading Mr. Fipps's address, thought Austin Friars sounded 'Ghostly'. The office of Mr. Fipps was in *a very dark passage on the first floor, oddly situated at the back of a house, across some leads.* MARTIN CHUZZLEWIT CH. XXXIX

The small boy (Dickens) *roaming down into Austin Friars wondered how the Friars used to like it.* . . . MISCELLANEOUS PAPERS: GONE ASTRAY

Ball's Pond *There is a hush through Mr. Dombey's house . . . the child lies, calm and beautiful, upon his little bed . . . in the City . . . there is not much business done . . . Perch, the messenger, stays long upon his errands; and finds himself in bars of public houses . . . holding forth upon the uncertainty of human affairs. . . . He goes home to Ball's Pond earlier in the evening than usual and treats Mrs. Perch to a veal cutlet and Scotch ale.* . . . DOMBEY AND SON CH. XVIII

From Ball's Pond, Mr. Perch brings Mrs. Perch to spend the day with Mr. Dombey's servants . . . on Dombey's second wedding day. DOMBEY AND SON CH. XXXI

Bank of England . . . *they passed into an office* (Consols Office, Bank of England) *where their business was to be transacted . . . 'Wot are them gen'l'men a settin' behind the counters?' asked the hoarse coachman. 'Reduced counsels, I s'pose', replied Mr. Weller . . . 'Wy, you don't suppose the reduced counsels is alive, do you?' inquired Sam . . . 'Wot are they, then?' 'Clerks', replied Sam.* PICKWICK PAPERS CH. LV

The personage who conducted the mysterious child of the feminine gender to church might be seen at the Bank of England about Dividend times. UNCOMMERCIAL TRAVELLER: CITY OF LONDON CHURCHES; THE DICKENSIAN, SPRING 1948: THE CITY CHURCHES

To walk on to the Bank, lamenting the good old times and bemoaning the present evil period, would be an easy next step, so I take it, and would make my houseless circuit of the Bank and give a thought to the treasure within; likewise to the guard of soldiers passing the night there, and nodding over the fire. UNCOMMERCIAL TRAVELLER: NIGHT WALKS

It would appear that Mr. Nicodemus Dumps took an extended lunch time from the Bank of England for the christening of his nephew's first child in Bloomsbury, for the purpose of acting as godfather. SKETCHES BY BOZ: BLOOMSBURY CHRISTENING

Hugh (once of the Maypole Inn), a great figure bareback on a horse, himself twice led an attack on the Bank of England, which failed. But since the riots of 1780 the Bank of England has a small military guard each night. BARNABY RUDGE CH. LXVII

When Tom Pinch was lost in London he decided to ask no one for directions *unless, indeed, he should happen to find himself near . . . the Bank of England; in which case he would step in, and ask a civil question or two, confiding in the perfect respectability of the concern.* MARTIN CHUZZLEWIT CH. XXXVII

If Bella thought as she glanced at the mighty Bank, how agreeable it would be to have an hour's gardening there, with a bright copper shovel among the money, still she was not in an avaricious vein. OUR MUTUAL FRIEND BOOK iii, CH. XVI

Mr Morfin . . . had a paternal affection for his violoncello which was once in every week transported from Islington, his place of abode, to a certain clubroom hard by the Bank, where quartettes of the most tormenting and excruciating nature were executed every Wednesday evening by a private party. DOMBEY AND SON CH. XIII

Barbican Oliver and Sikes pass this way en route for Chertsey. OLIVER TWIST CH. XXI

Clennam and Doyce parted here; the former, reaching St. Paul's, met John Baptist who had been knocked down and was being taken to St. Bartholomew's Hospital. LITTLE DORRIT BOOK i, CH. XIII

Here was the meeting place of the 'Prentice Knights in cellars along this thoroughfare, *profoundly dark, unpaved and reeking with stagnant odours. Into this ill-favoured pit, the locksmith's vagrant 'prentice groped his way.* BARNABY RUDGE CH. VIII

Barnard's Inn (Holborn). Here Pip and Herbert Pocket had chambers. On first sight Pip thought Barnard's Inn *the dingiest collection of shabby buildings ever squeezed together in a*

rank corner as a club for Tom-cats. GREAT EXPECTATIONS
CH. XXI

Included by the Uncommercial with the rest of the Inns
as *the shabby crew.* UNCOMMERCIAL TRAVELLER: CHAMBERS

Bank of England

Bartholomew's Close Awaiting Mr. Jaggers's arrival Pip
saw him coming across the road and towards his office; he
then saw the popularity and power of this lawyer by his
peremptory method of disposing of the several waiting
around to see him and their submissive acceptance of his
curt dismissal of them. GREAT EXPECTATIONS CH. XX

Battle Bridge This area has been known as King's Cross
since 1830. In the story, Mr. Boffin told Silas Wegg, *Where
I live is called The Bower, Boffin's Bower,* and directing him,
*when you've got nigh upon about a odd mile, or say and a quarter if
you like, up Maiden Lane, Battle Bridge, ask for Harmony
Jail.* Maiden Lane is now known as York Way. The
Wilfers lived beyond this area, in Holloway. OUR MUTUAL
FRIEND BOOK i, CH. V

The men who play the bells (apparently street entertainers)
have got scent of the marriage (Mr. Dombey's to Edith) *and
. . . are practising in a back settlement near Battlebridge.* DOMBEY
AND SON CH. XXXI

Mr. Blathers, one of the two officers from Bow Street,

investigating the burglary in Chertsey, entertains Rose Maylie, while partaking of some refreshments, with a story about a robbery in a public house *over Battlebridge way.* OLIVER TWIST CH. XXXI

Boz, speculating on the one-time myth of romance surrounding child sweeps, remembered *a little sweep about our own age with curly hair and white teeth, whom we devoutly and sincerely believed to be the lost son and heir of some illustrious personage,* who finally *settled down as a master sweep in the neighbourhood of Battle Bridge.* It would appear that the sweeps' dance on May Day was outstanding, but it and all such May Day celebrations were fading out. In search of relics of them, Boz *turned back down Maiden Lane with the intention of passing through the extensive colony lying between it and Battle Bridge, which is inhabited by proprietors of donkey carts, boilers of horse flesh, makers of tiles and sifters of cinders.* SKETCHES BY BOZ: FIRST OF MAY

Bayham Street The Dickens family lived for a year (1823) at No. 16 Bayham Street on first coming to London from the Rochester/Chatham area. The house was demolished in 1910. The Bayham Street days had sad memories for Dickens, for he had left a kindly schoolmaster at Chatham and no school had yet been found for him in London. LIFE

Bob Cratchit lived in Camden Town and it is thought probable that Dickens had his Bayham Street home in mind when he wrote of this family. A CHRISTMAS CAROL, STAVE ONE

It is also possible that Traddles lodged in the Bayham Street house with the Micawbers. *I found that the street was not as desirable a one as I could have wished it to be, for the sake of Traddles.* Traddles had told David Copperfield that he *lived in a little street near the Veterinary College at Camden Town.* DAVID COPPERFIELD CH. XXVII

Later, Traddles had to tell David that an execution had been put into the house (that presumed in Bayham Street) that Micawber had changed his name to Mortimer and the family had moved; he himself had been *living in a furnished apartment.* DAVID COPPERFIELD CH. XXXIV

Bedford Row Included by the Uncommercial as *replete with the accommodations of Solitude, Closeness and Darkness, where you might be as easily murdered, with the placid reputation of having merely gone down to the sea side.* UNCOMMERCIAL TRAVELLER: CHAMBERS

Bedford Square Horatio was compelled to admit having exchanged cards with Delafontaine of Bedford Square, and of having *had an opportunity of serving him considerably.* SKETCHES BY BOZ: HORATIO SPARKINS

Bedford Street The Civil Service Stores at the corner of Bedford Street and the Strand occupies the site of the factory in which David Copperfield so dexterously covered the tops of the blacking pots in sight of the public. This was Warren's Blacking Factory, moved from Hungerford Stairs. LIFE

Belgrave Square *Sitting, on a bright September morning, among my books and papers at my open window on the cliff overhanging the sea-beach* (Broadstairs?) *... I remember to have been in a City ... not long ago either, that was in the dreariest condition ... I walked through gloomy streets where every house was shut up and newspapered, and where my solitary footsteps echoed on the deserted pavements. In Belgrave Square I met the last man – an ostler – sitting on a post in a ragged, red waistcoat, eating straw, and mildewing away.* REPRINTED PIECES: OUT OF TOWN

In this district Cadogan Place is said to be the link between *the aristocratic pavements of Belgrave Square and the barbarism of Chelsea,* and here, in Cadogan Place, lived Mrs. Wititterly. NICHOLAS NICKLEBY CH. XXI

Belgravia (between Sloane Street, Hyde Park Corner and Grosvenor Place). Lady Tippins *that charmer ... dwelt over a staymaker's in the Belgravian Borders, with a life-size model in the window on the ground floor of a distinguished beauty in a blue petticoat, stay-lace in hand, looking over her shoulder at the town in innocent surprise. As well she may, to find herself dressing under the circumstances.* OUR MUTUAL FRIEND BOOK ii, CH. III

Bell Alley (now Mason's Avenue), Coleman Street. *Namby, Bell Alley, Coleman Street,* was the sheriff's office and to his house Mr. Pickwick was taken prior to being put into the Fleet Prison. PICKWICK PAPERS CH. XL

Bell Yard, Carter Lane. Dickens rented an office at No. 5, Bell Yard, off Carter Lane, in 1831 whilst a reporter for one of the Proctor's offices in the Doctors' Commons. LIFE

Bell Yard, Fleet Street. *Name of Neckett,* said the boy . . . *Bell Yard, Chandler's shop, left-hand side, name of Blinder.* Thus Mr. Jarndyce and his companions found Neckett's orphaned children, two locked in a garret, while the third washed and charred for their living, a pathetic story uncomplainingly told by the girl 'Charlie', her two charges lovingly clinging to her. BLEAK HOUSE CH. XV

Belle Sauvage, Ludgate Hill. Now gone, site cleared. Here stood the famous coaching Inn. The advent of railways undermined its importance, so it was removed in 1837. According to Sam Weller, his father, over-persuaded by a marriage licence tout and asked for his parish, answered 'Bell Savage' *for he stopped there when he drove up, and he knowed nothing about parishes, he didn't.* PICKWICK PAPERS CH. X

When Tony Weller, coachman, became widowed a second time, he told his son that rather than stay at home *to be married vether I vant to or not . . . I have come to the determination o' drivin' the Safety, and puttin' up vunce more at the Bell Savage, vich is my nat'ral-born element, Sammy.* PICKWICK PAPERS CH. LII

Bentinck Street, W1. At No. 18 (rebuilt), the Dickens family lived in 1833. LIFE

Berners Street *Another very different person who stopped our growth, we associate with Berners Street, Oxford Street. . . . The White Woman is her name. She is dressed entirely in white, with a ghastly white plaiting round her head and face, inside her white*

bonnet. . . . *She is a conceited old creature, cold and formal in manner, and evidently went simpering mad on personal grounds alone – no doubt because a wealthy Quaker wouldn't marry her. This is her bridal dress. She is always walking up here, on her way to church to marry the false Quaker. We observe in her mincing step and fishy eye that she intends to lead him a sharp life. We stopped growing when we got at the conclusion that the Quaker had had a happy escape of the White Woman.* (A possible source of Miss Havisham in GREAT EXPECTATIONS.) MISCELLANEOUS PAPERS: WHERE WE STOPPED GROWING

Bethlehem Hospital (now Imperial War Museum). *I chose next to wander by Bethlehem Hospital . . . partly, because I had a night fancy in my head. . . . Are not the sane and the insane equal at night as the sane lie a dreaming? . . . Are we not nightly persuaded . . . that we associate . . . with kings and queens. . . . Do we not nightly jumble events and personages. . . . Are we not sometimes troubled . . . to account for them . . . as these do sometimes in respect of their waking delusions? Said an afflicted man to me . . . 'Sir, I can frequently fly'. I was half ashamed to reflect that so could I – by night!* UNCOMMERCIAL TRAVELLER: NIGHT WALKS

Bethnal Green Down in Bethnal Green the Uncommercial's interest is riveted on a family of fowls, who seem to believe that everything came into existence for subservience to themselves, in conflict with which the lord of the family is afflicted with a paucity of feather and the lady with the appearance of *a bundle of office pens.* Goods vans that run over them leave them unharmed, miscellaneous objects as kettles and saucepans flung at them appear to them as merely something to peck at. Gaslight seems their natural aura, so that they begin to crow when public houses open up. UN-COMMERCIAL TRAVELLER: SHY NEIGHBOURHOODS

Beulah Spa A place of recreation with a maze at Norwood, opened in 1831. Now built over. *The Gordian knot was all very well in its way: So is the Maze at the Beulah Spa.* Thus Boz on the construction of Seven Dials. SKETCHES BY BOZ: SEVEN DIALS

Mr. Watkins Tottle, Mr. Timson and Miss Lillerton made up a small party in the course of their plans to go to Beulah Spa, which, however, never came off. SKETCHES BY BOZ: PASSAGE IN THE LIFE OF MR. WATKINS TOTTLE.

Bevis Marks Sampson Brass *was an attorney of no very good repute, from Bevis Marks in the City of London.* OLD CURIOSITY SHOP CH. XI

. . . *the historian takes the friendly reader by the hand, and springing with him into the air, and cleaving the same at a greater rate than ever Don Cleophas Leandro Perez Zambullo and his familiar travelled through that pleasant region in company, alights with him upon the pavement of Bevis Marks. The intrepid aeronauts alight before a small dark house . . . in the parlour window . . . there hung . . . a curtain of faded green. A rickety table with spare bundles of papers, yellow and ragged from long carriage in the pocket . . . a couple of stools set face to face on opposite sides of this crazy piece of furniture; a treacherous old chair . . . whose withered arms had hugged full many a client and helped to squeeze him dry; a second-hand wigbox, used as a depository for blank writs and declarations . . . a jar of ink, a pounce box . . . a carpet trodden to shreds but still clinging with the tightness of desperation to its tacks – these, with the yellow wainscot of the walls, the smoke discoloured ceiling, the dust and cobwebs, were among the most prominent decorations of the office of Mr. Sampson Brass.* OLD CURIOSITY SHOP CH. XXXIII

In a letter to Forster in 1840, Dickens wrote *I intended calling on you this morning on my way back from Bevis Marks whither I went to look at a house for Sampson Brass. But I got mingled up in a kind of social hash with the Jews of Houndsditch, and roamed about among them till I came out in Moorfields quite unexpectedly.* LIFE

The Red Lion in Bevis Marks (demolished) was generally considered to be the hostelry referred to by Dick Swiveller when he stated, *there is exceedingly mild porter in the immediate vicinity.* OLD CURIOSITY SHOP CH. XXXIV

Billingsgate One of the many places in which a job was found by Tip. LITTLE DORRIT BOOK i, CH. VII

Pip records passing *Old Billingsgate market* as he, Herbert and Startop made their anxious way in preparation to picking Magwitch up and so on by the river by which the latter was to escape recapture, with Pip for his faithful companion. GREAT EXPECTATIONS CH. LIV

The Uncommercial, wandering to escape sleeplessness, *went to Billingsgate, in some hope of market people*, but he was too early. UNCOMMERCIAL TRAVELLER: NIGHT WALKS

Bishopsgate Where Brogley, the broker, kept a shop in which *every description of second-hand furniture was exhibited in the most uncomfortable aspect.* DOMBEY AND SON CH. IX

Mr. Augustus Minns, invited to dinner by his cousin, Mr. Octavius Budden, is advised: *Now mind the direction the coach goes from the Flower Pot, in Bishopsgate, every half hour.* SKETCHES BY BOZ: MR. MINNS AND HIS COUSIN

Black Lion (demolished). At No. 75 Whitechapel Road, where Joe Willet partook of a frugal meal and spurning his father's advice to go up the Monument, left instead for the Blacksmith's house, attracted by the eyes of blooming Dolly Varden. BARNABY RUDGE CH. XIII

Blackfriars Bridge (1769–1863). The present bridge was opened in 1869. *I walked to and fro daily between Southwark and Blackfriars* (to and from the bottle washing warehouse) David Copperfield said, and Dickens recalled, writing of much that was his own experience, going from the Blacking Warehouse, across the Bridge, left down Union Street to Marshalsea Prison and his own lodgings in Lant Street. DAVID COPPERFIELD CH. XI; LIFE

We were not far from Blackfriars Bridge, David says, when he and Mr. Peggotty caught sight of Martha, whom they followed, and eventually saved, possibly from the river, entrusting her instead with an undertaking to find and help little Em'ly. DAVID COPPERFIELD CH. XLVI

One of the routes by which the rioters were to make their way, that is, over Blackfriars Bridge, and thus to the House of Commons. BARNABY RUDGE CH. XLIX

Hugh, of the Maypole, among other damage for which he

was responsible, helped to break open the toll-houses on Blackfriars Bridge and cast the money on to the street. BARNABY RUDGE CH. LXVII

Jo moves on, through the long vacation, down to Blackfriars Bridge, where he finds a baking, stony corner wherein to settle to his repast. BLEAK HOUSE CH. XIX

At first, Pip *kept above Blackfriars Bridge* in his daily practice in preparation for helping Magwitch to escape, and to accustom any watching his apparently harmless purpose. GREAT EXPECTATIONS CH. XLVI

Blackfriars Road *There was a long-legged young man with a very little empty donkey-cart, standing near the Obelisk, in the Blackfriars Road* (now in front of Imperial War Museum, Lambeth Road), *whose eye I caught as I was going by, and who, addressing me as 'Six penn'orth of bad ha'pence', hoped 'I should know him again to swear to' – in allusion, I have no doubt, to my staring at him.* David decided to employ him to convey his box to the Dover Coach office for sixpence and he made off with the little boy's box, so David had to walk all the way to Dover and his Aunt, Betsey Trotwood. DAVID COPPERFIELD CH. XII

Blackheath When little David Copperfield was sent to school it was to Salem House, down by Blackheath, *a square brick building with wings, of a bare and unfurnished appearance.* The school has never been located, although it was thought to be based on Wellington House Academy, Hampstead Road, attended by Dickens. DAVID COPPERFIELD CH. V

David, forced to carry out his plan to go to Dover on foot, having lost his trunk and half guinea, began his walk without delay and arriving on Blackheath, decided to pass the night *behind the wall at the back of my old school, in a corner where there used to be a haystack. I imagined it would be a kind of company to have the boys, and the bedroom where I used to tell the stories, so near to me.* DAVID COPPERFIELD CH. XIII

David Copperfield, going by coach from Canterbury to London on the first stage of a month's holiday, on the advice of his Aunt, *to look about him,* and decide on a future career, passed Salem House where Mr. Creakle had laid about him with a heavy hand – *I would have given all I had for lawful permission to get down and thrash him and let all the boys out like so many caged sparrows.* DAVID COPPERFIELD CH. XIX

John Rokesmith and his wife had *a modest little cottage, but bright and fresh,* on Blackheath. OUR MUTUAL FRIEND BOOK IV CH. IV

On his walk from Rochester to London – the last part of which he did by rail from Greenwich (the first railway in London), Dickens says, *Christmas begirt me, far and near, until I had come to Blackheath, and had walked down the long vista of gnarled old trees in Greenwich Park.* . . . CHRISTMAS STORIES: SEVEN POOR TRAVELLERS; LIFE

On his way by travelling chariot abroad, the Uncommercial came on Blackheath. He met and took up the *very small, queer boy,* and the conversation about Falstaff, Gads Hill, took place, the latter part a memory of Charles Dickens about a walk with his father. UNCOMMERCIAL TRAVELLER: TRAVELLING ABROAD

The Dover Mail, ascending Shooter's Hill, Blackheath, on *that Friday night in November, one thousand seven hundred and seventy five,* when *the guard suspected the passengers, the passengers suspected one another and the guard . . . and the coachman was sure of nothing but the horses,* is a typical illustration of what travellers in those days had to expect, especially on such roads as those over Blackheath. A TALE OF TWO CITIES CH. II

Cobbs remarked that *Master Harry Walmers' father, you see, he lived at the Elmses, downaway by Shooter's Hill there, six or seven miles from Lunnon.* CHRISTMAS STORIES: THE HOLLY TREE

Tony Weller retired on a handsome independence to *an excellent public house near Shooter's Hill, where he is quite reverenced as an oracle.* PICKWICK PAPERS CH. LVII

On Shooter's Hill stands Severndroog Castle, built by Lady James in 1784. *Away they go . . . to catch a glimpse of the rich cornfields and beautiful orchards of Kent; or to stroll among the fine old trees of Greenwich Park, and survey the wonders of Shooter's Hill and Lady James's Folly.* REPRINTED PIECES: SUNDAY UNDER THREE HEADS

Bleeding Heart Yard (Turning out of Greville (previously Charles) Street.) Where the Plornish family lived. *You got into it down a flight of steps . . . and got out of it by a low gateway into a maze of shabby streets. . . . At this end of the Yard and over the gateway was the factory of Daniel Doyce.* LITTLE DORRIT BOOK i, CH. XII

Bloomsbury The parish in which Nicodemus Dumps, the most miserable man in the world, lived. *He adored King Herod for his massacre of the innocents.* He attended the christening of his nephew's first child, a boy, and ruined the occasion by his tactless remarks. The christening took place at the church of St. George, Hart Street, now Bloomsbury Way. SKETCHES BY BOZ: THE BLOOMSBURY CHRISTENING

Bloomsbury Square In this Square was Lord Mansfield's house, No. 29, burnt by the Gordon rioters, whereby furniture, plate and jewels, manuscripts, a gallery of pictures and the great Law Library were lost to the world. *Two cripples – both mere boys – were hanged in this same Bloomsbury Square,* their misery protracted while they were made to turn and face Lord Mansfield's house, which they had helped to ruin. BARNABY RUDGE CH. LXXVII

A correspondent writes to Master Humphrey of a charming fellow who had performed the feat six times of carrying away every bell handle in Bloomsbury Square. MASTER HUMPHREY'S CLOCK CH. I

Blue Boar, Aldgate. See Aldgate.

Blue Boar, Gracechurch Street. See Leadenhall Market.

Bond Street *Along one of the thoroughfares which lie between Park Lane and Bond Street,* Nicholas stopped at a handsome hotel for *a pint of wine and a biscuit,* and in the coffee room heard the disparaging conversation between Sir Mulberry Hawk and Lord Frederick Verisopht concerning *little Kate Nickleby,* which resulted in the fight between Nicholas and Mulberry Hawk. NICHOLAS NICKLEBY CH. XXXII

Long's Hotel in Bond Street, at which Cousin Feenix used to stay, was at No. 15 New Bond Street. DOMBEY AND SON CH. XXXI

After Florence and Walter have been married a year, and the former is reconciled with her father and his recovery slowly progresses, Florence is beguiled by Cousin Feenix to drive to Brook Street, off Bond Street, where Mr. Dombey's marriage to Edith had been celebrated. Florence and Edith meet again, to effect a sad reconciliation, as Cousin Feenix had hoped by his strategy. DOMBEY AND SON CH. LXI

Of the district between Savile Row, Burlington Gardens and Old Bond Street, Dickens wrote *I have taken a lodging for six weeks in the most unfrequented part of England – in a word, in London. The retreat into which I have withdrawn myself is Bond Street. From this lonely spot I make pilgrimages into the surrounding wilderness, and traverse extensive tracts of the Great Desert.* UNCOMMERCIAL TRAVELLER: ARCADIAN LONDON; THE DICKENSIAN, AUTUMN 1949

On a shopping expedition Mrs. Malderton and her daughters *made their second call at Redmayne's in Bond Street.* SKETCHES BY BOZ: HORATIO SPARKINS

Borough Market

Boot Tavern, Cromer Street. At No. 116 the Boot Tavern stands on the site of the old Boot described as a *lone house of*

public entertainment, situated in the fields at the back of the Foundling Hospital; a very solitary spot at that period, and quite deserted after dark. The tavern stood at some distance from any high road and was approachable only by a dark and narrow lane. BARNABY RUDGE CH. XXXVIII

Borough While Alfred Jingle was on his way back from Doctors' Commons, Sam Weller was *burnishing a pair of painted tops* belonging to a farmer *who was refreshing himself with a slight lunch of two or three pounds of cold beef and a pot or two of porter, after the fatigues of the Borough Market.* PICKWICK PAPERS CH. X

Mr. Bob Allen, returning from seeing Mr. Pickwick on his way home after the party in Lant Street, *knocked double knocks at the door of the Borough Market Office, and took short naps*

George Inn, Borough

on the steps alternately, until daybreak, under the firm impression that he lived there and had forgotten the key. PICKWICK PAPERS CH. XXXII

White Hart Yard (on left, after passing St. Thomas Street) marks the site of the White Hart Inn (demolished in 1889), where Mr. Pickwick found Sam Weller. It was here also that Mr. Pickwick and Mr. Wardle found Jingle and Rachael Wardle, after their elopement. PICKWICK PAPERS CH. X

The George Inn (next yard but one on the left) is the only remaining galleried inn in London, of which there were some half dozen still left at the time of PICKWICK PAPERS. It was here that Tip Dorrit wrote a begging letter to Arthur Clennam. LITTLE DORRIT BOOK i, CH. XXII

Gashford was found dead in his bed at an obscure inn in the Borough where he was quite unknown. BARNABY RUDGE CH. LXXXII

Whosoever goes into Marshalsea Place (now gone) *turning out of Angel Court* (now Place), *leading to Bermondsey, will find his feet on the very paving-stones of the extinct Marshalsea Jail.* LITTLE DORRIT, PREFACE. John Dickens was held here for debt. LIFE. Mr. William Dorrit was here for many years. Little Dorrit was born in the Marshalsea. LITTLE DORRIT BOOK i, CH. VI, VIII, IX, XXXVI

Mr. F's Aunt sat on the steps of the Marshal's official residence, *a great boon to the younger inhabitants of the Borough, whose sallies of humour she had considerably flushed herself by resent-*

Site of Marshalsea, Borough

ing, at the point of her umbrella. LITTLE DORRIT BOOK ii, CH. XXXIV.

The Marshalsea (not Debtor's Prison) 1376–1811 was on the same side of the Borough, nearer to London Bridge (site marked by plaque). Little Dorrit was christened at St. George's Church and one night, when shut out of the Prison, where she lived, rested in the vestry. At the end of the story she was married here to Arthur Clennam. LITTLE DORRIT BOOK i, CH. VII, XIV; BOOK ii, CH. XXXIV

King's Bench Prison stood at the corner of the Borough Road, near St. George's Church. Here Mr. Micawber was imprisoned for debt, Dickens using many incidents relating to his father in the Marshalsea. DAVID COPPERFIELD CH. XI, XII, XLIX. 'The Rules' of the King's Bench Prison was a district about three miles in circumference around the prison, where the more favoured debtors lived. Here Madeleine Bray lived with her father. She was later married to Nicholas Nickleby. NICHOLAS NICKLEBY CH. XLVI

Lant Street – Dickens lived in Lant Street as a boy, when his father was in the Marshalsea. He used his landlord and landlady as models for the characters of Mr. and Mrs. Garland in THE OLD CURIOSITY SHOP. He also used his lodgings for David Copperfield, when Mr. Micawber was in the King's Bench Prison. LIFE; DAVID COPPERFIELD CH. XI

St. George's Church, Borough

There's my lodgings, said Mr. Bob Sawyer, producing a card, *Lant Street, Borough; it's near Guy's and handy for me, you know. Little distance after you've passed St. George's Church – turns out of the High Street, on the right-hand side of the way.* PICKWICK PAPERS CH. XXX

There is a repose about Lant Street, in the Borough, which sheds a gentle melancholy upon the soul. There are always a good many houses to let in the street; it is a by-street, too, and its dulness is soothing. The majority of the inhabitants either direct their energies to the letting of furnished apartments, or devote themselves to the healthful and invigorating pursuit of mangling. The chief features in the still life of the street are green shutters, lodging-bills, brass door-plates, and bell-handles; the principal specimens of animated nature, the pot-boy, the muffin youth, and the baked-potato man. The population is migratory, usually disappearing on the verge of quarter-day, and generally by night. Her Majesty's revenues are seldom collected in this happy valley; the rents are dubious; and the water communication is very frequently cut off. Thus runs the famous description of this street, which has been largely rebuilt. PICKWICK PAPERS CH. XXXII

The Borough is also mentioned in REPRINTED PIECES: ON DUTY WITH INSPECTOR FIELD, and in UNCOMMERCIAL TRAVELLER: NIGHT WALKS

Borough Clink On one night in the week of the Gordon riots, *In two hours, six-and-thirty fires were raging – six-and-thirty great conflagrations. Among them the Borough Clink in Tooley Street* (not rebuilt). BARNABY RUDGE CH. LXVII

Boswell Court, WC1. Residence of Mr. Loggins, the solicitor who was invited to the Steam Excursion but sent back an excuse. SKETCHES BY BOZ: STEAM EXCURSION

Bow On engaging Nicholas the Cheeryble Brothers suggested letting him *that little cottage at Bow which is empty,* at first for nothing but on consideration – *Perhaps it would be better,* Mr. Charles suggested, *to say something . . . it would help to preserve habits of frugality,* and a small sum was agreed, to be made up in some other way, which was most generously managed. NICHOLAS NICKLEBY CH. XXXV

Comparing the fineness of the day favourably in contrast to out of town, Tim Linkinwater said, *You should see it from my bedroom window.*

You should see it from mine, replies Nicholas . . . *Pooh, pooh,* said Tim Linkinwater . . . *Country!* (Bow was quite a rustic place to Tim) as, comparatively, it was in those days! NICHOLAS NICKLEBY CH. XL

Bow Church (St. Mary-le-Bow). . . . *The offices of Dombey & Son were within the liberties of the City of London and within hearing of Bow Bells, when their clashing voices were not drowned by the uproar in the streets.* DOMBEY AND SON CH. IV

Bow Street Police Court (The Police Court of Dickens's day was on the other side of Bow Street between Russell

Street and Covent Garden Theatre.) At which the Artful Dodger appeared, accused of taking a handkerchief out of an old gentleman's pocket. Finding it an old one, he returned it, only to be caught for it by a police officer, and subsequently found to have a silver snuff box in his pocket, with the true owner's name engraved upon the lid. OLIVER TWIST CH. XLIII

Barnaby, taken prisoner in the riots, was first taken to Bow Street Police Court and questioned, to no effect; he was marched to Newgate, where heavy irons were riveted on him, and so left, but Grip (his pet raven), unseen by him at first, was thrust in with him. BARNABY RUDGE CH. LVIII

Walking up Bow Street, on his way to the first performance on Saturday as compared with the Sunday performance given in the Britannia Theatre, Dickens found it and surrounding streets so dull, looking *broken and bankrupt, that the 'Found Dead' on the black board at the police station might have announced the decease of the Drama.* See Britannia Theatre. UNCOMMERCIAL TRAVELLER: TWO VIEWS OF A CHEAP THEATRE

David and Dora kept a page, all other domestics failing, who stole Dora's watch and on the proceeds went up and down between London

Bow Church (St. Mary-le-Bow)

and Uxbridge on a coach. On the fifteenth journey he was caught and taken to Bow Street. DAVID COPPERFIELD CH. XLVIII

Pip's sister, Mrs. Joe Gargery, was struck down with the convict's leg iron, which Joe later declared to be an old one, and Pip felt sure was the one 'his' convict, Magwitch, had filed off with a file he had taken to him. *The Constables and the Bow Street men from London . . . were about the house for a week or two.* GREAT EXPECTATIONS CH. XVI

We were passing the corner of Bow Street . . . when a crowd assembled round the door of the Police Office, attracted our attention. Two girls, sixteen and fourteen, had been charged and sent off in *Her Majesty's carriage* for *six weeks and labour,* as the elder defiantly told a questioner on their return to the van. SKETCHES BY BOZ: PRISONERS' VAN

Brentford Oliver and Bill Sikes went through Brentford en route for Chertsey. OLIVER TWIST CH. XXI

Arthur lived at the top of Compeyson's house (over nigh Brentford it was), and Compeyson kept a careful account agen him for board and lodging. From Magwitch's account to Pip concerning the man who was to have married Miss Havisham. GREAT EXPECTATIONS CH. XLII

The abode of Mrs. Betty Higden was not easy to find, lying in such complicated back settlements of muddy Brentford that they left their equipage at the sign of the Three Magpies and went in search of it on foot. (The Three Magpies is identified with the Three Pigeons at Brentford.) OUR MUTUAL FRIEND BOOK i, CH. XVI

Brick Lane, Shoreditch. At No. 160 was a Mission Hall, generally accepted as the original of the famous one in PICKWICK PAPERS where we read that *The monthly meetings of the Brick Lane Branch of the United Grand Junction Ebenezer Temperance Association, were held in a large room, pleasantly and airily situated at the top of a safe and commodious ladder.* Previous to the commencement of business, the ladies sat upon forms and drank tea, till such time as they considered it expedient to leave off. PICKWICK PAPERS CH. XXXIII

Bridewell (Workhouse, House of Correction and Reformatory near Blackfriars. Demolished in 1864.) Miss Miggs was chosen out of one hundred and twenty four competitors by Justices of the Peace for Middlesex to be female turnkey for the County Bridewell, an office she held till her death more than thirty years after. BARNABY RUDGE CH. LXXXII

Noah taunts Oliver with innuendoes against his mother, such as *it's a great deal better, Work'us, that she died when she did, or else she'd have been hard labouring in Bridewell, or transported, or hung.* This led to Oliver assaulting the bully and finally, with all his force, felling him to the ground. From this event came a great change in Oliver's life. OLIVER TWIST CH. VI

Brig Place Captain Cuttle lodged with a Mrs. McStinger at No. 9 Brig Place. He *lived on the brink of a little canal, near the India Docks, where there was a swivel bridge which opened now and then to let some wandering monster of a ship come roaming up the street like a stranded leviathan.* DOMBEY AND SON CH. IX

It is thought that Brig Place was at the Limehouse end of the City Canal, opened in 1812, constructed for the purpose of saving ships under sail the long beat round the Isle of Dogs, cutting across the upper part of this curious tongue of land, measuring about three quarters of a mile across from the Blackwall Reach to Limehouse Reach. As there was a toll, ships' masters boycotted the little Canal, which was eventually absorbed into the West India Docks system. Behind the City Arms at the Limehouse end (rebuilt) a few houses were to be seen, old but too tall for the two-storied Brig Place dwellings of the McStinger era, and an open space in which one could trace where the swivel bridge let in a *roaming monster of a ship* now and then, while high palings allowed one to see through cracks the length of the Canal itself. THE DICKENSIAN, SUMMER 1935: CAPTAIN CUTTLE'S LODGINGS

Britannia Theatre, Hoxton Street (demolished in Air Raid 1940). *The stage itself, and all its appurtenances . . . are on a scale more like the Scala at Milan . . . the Grand Opera at Paris, than any notion a stranger would be likely to form of the Britannia Theatre at Hoxton, a mile north of St. Luke's Hospital in the Old Street Road, London.* UNCOMMERCIAL TRAVELLER: TWO VIEWS OF A CHEAP THEATRE

British Museum Dickens as a young man was an assiduous attendant at its reading rooms. LIFE

In the British Museum there is a curious pamphlet got up by the Agnews of Charles's time, entitled 'A Divine Tragedie lately acted ... upon Sabbath Breakers ... worthy to be knowne and considered of all men'. REPRINTED PIECES: SUNDAY UNDER THREE HEADS: 'AS IT MIGHT BE MADE'

We were once haunted by a shabby-genteel man. . . . He first attracted our notice, by sitting opposite us in the reading-room of the British Museum. SKETCHES BY BOZ: SHABBY-GENTEEL PEOPLE

... it had occurred to the busy little spouse of Tibbs, that the best thing she could do with a legacy of 700l. would be to take and furnish a tolerable house ... between the British Museum, and a remote village called Somers Town – for the reception of boarders. SKETCHES BY BOZ: THE BOARDING HOUSE

As to our women; – next Easter or Whitsuntide, look at the bonnets at the British Museum or the National Gallery, and think of the pretty white French cap, the Spanish mantilla or the Genoese mezzero. UNCOMMERCIAL TRAVELLER: THE BOILED BEEF OF NEW ENGLAND

Brixton The Medical Officer cites the case of a patient, who, on finding he had held an erroneous idea as to the locality of his stomach, *burst into tears, put out his hand, and said, 'Jobling, God bless you' . . . became speechless and was ultimately buried at Brixton.* MARTIN CHUZZLEWIT CH. XXVII

Brixton was one of the places in which Pickwick carried on his 'unwearied researches'. PICKWICK PAPERS CH. I

Concerning high winds *Brixton seems to have something on its conscience.* UNCOMMERCIAL TRAVELLER: REFRESHMENTS FOR TRAVELLERS

Broad Court *Snevellicci is my name. I'm to be found in Broad Court, Bow Street, when I'm in town.* NICHOLAS NICKLEBY CH. XXX

Brook Street Mrs. Skewton *borrowed a house in Brook Street, Grosvenor Square, from a stately relative* (one of the Feenix brood) *who was out of town,* and who did not mind letting her have the house for Edith's wedding to Mr. Dombey, *as the loan implied his final release and acquittance from all further loans and gifts to Mrs. Skewton and her daughter.* DOMBEY AND SON CH. XXX

In a hotel in Brook Street Mr. Dorrit resided in the days of his affluence and here the advent of the great Merdle to visit Mr. Dorrit caused much commotion in the office. LITTLE DORRIT BOOK ii, CH. XVI

Bryanston Square *Mr. Dombey's house was a large one, on the shady side of a tall, dark, dreadfully genteel street in the region between Portland Place and Bryanston Square. It was a corner house, with great wide areas containing cellars frowned upon by barred windows, and leered at by crooked-eyed doors leading to dustbins. It was a house of dismal state, with a circular back to it, containing a whole suite of drawing-rooms looking upon a gravelled yard, where two gaunt trees, with blackened trunks and branches rattled rather than rustled, their leaves were so smoke dried.* DOMBEY AND SON CH. III

Buckingham Palace 'Her Majesty was intensely interested to see 'The Frozen Deep' but felt that assent would involve either perpetual compliance in other requests or perpetually giving offence. She therefore suggested that Dickens select a room in Buckingham Palace and let her see the play there. Dickens objected that he *did not feel easy as to the social position* of his daughters at *a court under those circumstances*. It was finally arranged for the Queen to go to the Gallery of Illustration to a private performance for her and invited guests.' EDGAR JOHNSON: CHARLES DICKENS

In 1870, a few months before his death, Dickens was received at Buckingham Palace by Queen Victoria, who presented him with an autographed copy of her 'Journal of Our Life in the Highlands'. LIFE

Buckingham Street . . . *an advertisement . . . setting forth that in Buckingham Street, in the Adelphi there was to be let furnished, . . . a singularly desirable and compact set of chambers, forming a genteel residence for a young gentleman, a member of one of the Inns of Court, or otherwise. 'And a sweet set they is for sich'* said Mrs. *Crupp, the landlady.* DAVID COPPERFIELD CH. XXIII

Here Dickens himself lodged in 1833 or 1834. LIFE

Bull Inn, Aldgate. The Bull Inn stood on the spot now occupied by Aldgate Avenue until 1868. '*I shall work down to Ipswich the day arter tomorrow, sir*' *said Mr. Weller the elder,* '*from the Bull in Whitechapel; and if you really mean to go, you'd better go with me.*' PICKWICK PAPERS CH. XX

'*That 'ere your governor's luggage, Sammy?*' *inquired Mr. Weller ... as he entered the yard of the Bull Inn.... *'*The governor hisself'll be down here presently*'. '*He's a-cabbin' it, I suppose?*' *said the father.* '*Yes, he's a-havin' two mile o' danger at eight-pence*', *responded the son.* PICKWICK PAPERS CH. XXII

Bull Inn, Holborn. Formerly the Black Bull Inn and so called in Horwood's Map of 1799, published 1800. Gamages, Holborn is now on the site. Here Mrs. Gamp and Betsey Prig nursed Mr. Lewsome *turn and turn about,* meaning alternate day and night duties. MARTIN CHUZZLEWIT CH. XXV

Burlington Arcade, Piccadilly

Burlington Arcade Dickens wrote of the area between Burlington Arcade, Savile Row, Burlington Gardens and

Old Bond Street, too detailed for brief reference, but worth reading before visiting that still attractive area, especially the Arcade. UNCOMMERCIAL TRAVELLER: ARCADIAN LONDON. See also THE DICKENSIAN, AUTUMN 1949

Camberwell The Maldertons lived at Oak Lodge, Camberwell, where *any one who could lay claim to an acquaintance with people of rank and title, had a sure passport* to their table. SKETCHES BY BOZ: HORATIO SPARKINS

One of the several places in which Pickwick made his *Unwearied Researches.* PICKWICK PAPERS CH. I

Camberwell figures in the amusing account of Wemmick's wedding. *We went towards Camberwell Green, and when we were thereabouts, Wemmick said suddenly 'Halloa! Here's a church!' There was nothing very surprising in that; but again, I was rather surprised, when he said, as if he were animated by a brilliant idea, 'Let's go in!'. . . 'Halloa!' said Wemmick, 'Here's Miss Skiffins! Let's have a wedding!'* St. Giles Church, Camberwell, near the Green, is pointed out as the church referred to. GREAT EXPECTATIONS CH. LV

Mr. Wopsle had in his hand the affecting tragedy of George Barnwell, in which he had that moment invested sixpence, with a view of heaping every word of it on the head of Pumblechook, with whom he was going to drink tea. There follows an evening taken up as Wopsle intended, Pip a rather embarrassed participant. The Tragedy of George Barnwell, who lived in Camberwell, was a favourite one with Dickens as a boy, for recitations, and several references to it are made in the novels. GREAT EXPECTATIONS CH. XV; LIFE

Tom Pinch, and Mr. Pecksniff too, both visited the former's sister at a house in Camberwell, where she was a governess in a family *in a house so big and fierce, that its mere outside, like the outside of a giant's castle, struck terror into vulgar minds.* MARTIN CHUZZLEWIT CH. IX

Nicholas Nickleby happened to join the firm of Cheeryble Brothers, when he so pleased Tim Linkinwater with his sample of book-keeping and handwriting, on Tim's birthday. On these occasions the brothers were used to celebrating with a dinner party – themselves, Tim and his sister. On this occasion there had been some little anxiety about the non-arrival of the sister's cap, to come by messenger from the house in Camberwell where she was employed. However, after some risks taken by the messenger en route, the cap arrived safely and in time. NICHOLAS NICKLEBY CH. XXXVII

Camden Town (See also Bayham Street). *He lies concealed in a wretched lodging in Camden Town.* PICKWICK PAPERS CH. XXI

It was to Stagg's Gardens, Camden Town, known to the inhabitants as Camberling Town, that Richards, urged on by Susan Nipper and unknown to Mr. Dombey, went to see her family and especially the young Charitable Grinder, Number 147. This led to Florence getting lost, poor Richards losing her post and little Paul his foster mother. DOMBEY AND SON CH. VI

Miss Evans, *her maternal parent and two sisters, formed an harmonious quartett in the most secluded portion of Camden Town.* SKETCHES BY BOZ: MISS EVANS AND THE EAGLE

The building of the L. & N.W. Railway and the goods yard at Camden are described in MISCELLANEOUS PAPERS: AN UNSETTLED NEIGHBOURHOOD

Cannon Street Mr. Jinkins (at the Todgers' dinner party for the Pecksniffs) reminds them *that they have heard of a somewhat similar establishment in Cannon Street.* MARTIN CHUZZLEWIT CH. IX

Carlisle Street See Soho and Soho Square.

Castle Street (now Furnival Street). Traddles lodged *up behind the parapet of a house in Castle Street, Holborn.* DAVID COPPERFIELD CH. XXXVI

Cavendish Square *The lady's name ... is Mantalini – Madame Mantalini. ... She lives near Cavendish Square ... they arrived ... at the dressmaker's door, which displayed a very large plate with Madame Mantalini's name and occupation and was approached by a handsome flight of steps. ... Madame Mantalini's showrooms were on the first floor; a fact which was notified to the nobility and gentry, by the casual exhibition, near the handsomely curtained windows of two or three elegant bonnets ... and some costly garments in the most approved taste.* NICHOLAS NICKLEBY CH. X

Upon that establishment of state, the Merdle establishment in Harley Street, Cavendish Square, there was the shadow of no more common wall than the fronts of other establishments of state on the opposite side of the street. LITTLE DORRIT BOOK i, CH. XXI

Over against a London House, a corner house not far from Cavendish Square, a man with a wooden leg had sat for some years, with his remaining foot in a basket in cold weather, the evil genius, Silas Wegg. OUR MUTUAL FRIEND BOOK i, CH. V

Lord George Gordon rode *along the Strand ... and thence to his house in Welbeck Street, near Cavendish Square, whither he was attended by a few dozen idlers!* Lord George Gordon's house was No. 64, close to Wigmore Street (since rebuilt). BARNABY RUDGE CH. XXXVII

Cecil Street Here Dickens lodged in 1833. The site is covered by Shell-Mex House. LIFE

Watkins Tottle also lived here. *Fancy transformed his small parlour in Cecil Street, Strand, into a neat house in the suburbs.* SKETCHES BY BOZ: A PASSAGE IN THE LIFE OF MR. WATKINS TOTTLE

Chancery Lane John Rokesmith said, *Mr. Boffin, I happened to be in Chancery Lane this morning, when I saw you going along before me. I took the liberty of following you, trying to make up my mind to speak to you.* OUR MUTUAL FRIEND BOOK i, CH. VIII

Old Tom Jarndyce in despair blew his brains out at a coffee house in Chancery Lane, and Mrs. Snagsby was *the high standard of comparison among the neighbouring wives, a long way down Chancery Lane on both sides.* Young Smallweed had *a passion for a lady at a cigar shop* here, and Esther remarked to

Mr. Bucket, '*It looks like Chancery Lane.*' '*And was christened so, my dear*' *said* Mr. Bucket. Indeed, BLEAK HOUSE is the novel of Chancery Lane. In Cursitor Street on the left is Took's Court, the original of Cook's Court, where *Mr. Snagsby, Law-Stationer, pursues his lawful calling. In the shade of Cook's Court, at most times a shady place,* Mr. *Snagsby has dealt in all sorts of blank forms of legal process; in skins and rolls of parchment; in paper – foolscap, brief, draft, brown, white, whitey-brown, and blotting; in stamps, in office-quills, pens, ink, India-rubber, pounce, pins, pencils, sealing-wax and wafers; in red tape and green ferret; in pocket books, almanacks, diaries and law lists; in string, boxes, rulers, inkstands, glass and leaden penknives, scissors, bodkins, and other office cutlery!*

Mrs. Snagsby's own domain was the drawing room. *The view it commands of Cook's Court at one end (not to mention a squint into Cursitor Street), and of Coavinses', the sheriff's officer's back-yard at the other, she regards as a prospect of unequalled beauty.* BLEAK HOUSE CH. V, X, XX, XXXII, LI, LIX

See also Serjeant's Inn.

Charing Cross Mr. Haredale, during the Gordon riots, was refused refreshment at *an hotel near Charing Cross*; no name is given, but it is a sign of the antipathy to Catholics. BARNABY RUDGE CH. LXVI

An amusing story is told of being an hour too soon for the Birmingham High-flier coach from the Golden Cross (Charing Cross), of the wait and great activity a few minutes before the coach leaves; horses out, luggage stowed; paper boys yelling and the hot brandy and water the too-early traveller ordered, *served two minutes and a half before the time fixed for the starting of the coach*. SKETCHES BY BOZ: EARLY COACHES

At Charing Cross, Eugene Wrayburn witnessed the *ridiculous and feeble spectacle* of Jenny Wren's bad boy trying to cross the road. OUR MUTUAL FRIEND BOOK iii, CH. X

The Golden Cross Hotel in Pickwickian days stood on the spot where Nelson's monument now stands. It was rebuilt in 1831–32 but it was the old hotel Dickens referred to. It was from the older hostelry that the Pickwickians started for Rochester by coach, the old hotel having an archway in the rear, causing Jingle to cry: *Heads, heads – take care of your heads!* PICKWICK PAPERS CH. II

David Copperfield stayed here when deciding on a career – *We went to the Golden Cross at Charing Cross.* DAVID COPPERFIELD CH. XIX

It was also the old hostelry to which David took Mr. Peggotty after the meeting on St. Martin's church steps, and while talking to Peggotty, saw Martha hiding and listening in the half-closed door and knew it was her face he had seen just before he recognized Mr. Peggotty on the steps of the church. DAVID COPPERFIELD CH. XL

Cheapside Along Cheapside rode Lord George Gordon on his way home, solemnly acknowledging any who greeted his passing. BARNABY RUDGE CH. XXXVII

Five o'clock arriving, and with it Mr. Carker's bay horse, they (he and his teeth!) *got on horseback, and went gleaming up Cheapside.* DOMBEY AND SON CH. XXII

. . . *everybody that passed up Cheapside, and down Cheapside, looked wet, cold and dirty.* SKETCHES BY BOZ: THE BLOOMSBURY CHRISTENING

Arthur Clennam walked from Ludgate Hill and through some crooked streets lying between the river and Cheapside, on his way to his mother's. LITTLE DORRIT BOOK i, CH. III

Mr. Mould, the undertaker, lived *deep in the City, and within the ward of Cheap.* MARTIN CHUZZLEWIT CH. XXV

After calling on Dodson & Fogg, Sam and Mr. Pickwick walk down Cheapside where Mr. Pickwick has a glass of brandy and warm water and meets Sam's father, Tony Weller. PICKWICK PAPERS CH. XX

Mrs. Nickleby, discussing the distance to her lodgings with Lord Verisopht says . . . *all down Cheapside etc.* . . . NICHOLAS NICKLEBY CH. XXVI

Tim Linkinwater was suspected of having been seen walking down Cheapside with an uncommonly handsome spinster. NICHOLAS NICKLEBY CH. XXXVII

Because of his youthful appearance, Reginald Wilfer's schoolmaster meeting him in Cheapside might have been

tempted to cane him on the spot. OUR MUTUAL FRIEND BOOK i,
CH. IV. Riah went from St. Mary Axe to the Albany via
Cheapside, etc. OUR MUTUAL FRIEND BOOK iii, CH. I

Pip meets Mr. Jaggers in Cheapside and is invited to dine
with him. GREAT EXPECTATIONS CH. XLVIII

See also Cross Keys Inn.

Chelsea Mr. Kenge's cousin was a Mr. Bayham Badger, who
had a good practice at Chelsea. He was quite willing to
receive Richard into his house and to superintend his studies.
An agreement was made, the Lord Chancellor's consent
obtained, and it was settled. BLEAK HOUSE CH. XIII

Dickens lived in Selwood Terrace, Chelsea, prior to his
marriage to Catherine Hogarth at St. Luke's Church, Sydney
Street, Chelsea, on April 2nd, 1836. LIFE

. . . *few would venture . . . to Chelsea, unarmed and unattended;*
for fear of footpads. BARNABY RUDGE CH. XVI. The Royal
East London Volunteers, of which Gabriel Varden was a
member, marched to the Chelsea Bun-house. BARNABY
RUDGE CH. XLII. The Gordon Rioters announced their
intention of proceeding to Chelsea. BARNABY RUDGE CH. LIII

Miss Sophia Wackles, who was being courted by Dick
Swiveller, lived in Chelsea. OLD CURIOSITY SHOP CH. VIII

Crummles is NOT a Prussian, having been born in Chelsea. So
ran a newspaper cutting which Mr. Crummles showed to
Nicholas Nickleby. NICHOLAS NICKLEBY CH. XLVIII

Chelsea Water-works is nothin' to you. That was Sam Weller's
remark to Job Trotter who kept bursting into tears. PICK-
WICK PAPERS CH. XXIII

Tally-ho Thompson, a famous horse-stealer, lived with his
wife and little daughter at Chelsea. REPRINTED PIECES: THE
DETECTIVE POLICE

Chelsea Ferry Silas Wegg refers to this in his poem:
> *Then farewell, my trim-built wherry,*
> *Oars and coat and badge farewell!*
> *Never more at Chelsea Ferry,*
> *Shall your Thomas take a spell!*

OUR MUTUAL FRIEND BOOK i, CH. XV

Chertsey It was at a house in Chertsey that Bill Sikes and Toby Crackit committed the burglary and Oliver Twist was shot. The original *detached house surrounded by a wall* is thought to have been Pycroft House – now an Infant School. OLIVER TWIST CH. XXII

Chigwell The King's Head at Chigwell, opposite the Parish Church, is the original of The Maypole Inn, although its description calls upon the imagination – *an old building with more gable ends than a lazy man would care to count on a sunny day.* BARNABY RUDGE CH. I

Church Row, Limehouse (gone). At No. 5, Christopher Huffam, godfather of Charles Dickens, lived, *rigger in His Majesty's Navy,* and here the little boy of eleven would visit his godfather and doubtless his sail loft nearby and so gained some of his lore of ships, the sea and sailors. LIFE; THE DICKENSIAN, SUMMER 1935

Church Street, Smith Square (now Dean Stanley Street). Here the Doll's dressmaker, Jenny Wren, lived with her drunken father, her *bad boy* near *a certain little street, called Church Street, and a certain little blind square, called Smith Square, in the centre of which last retreat is a very hideous church, with four towers at the four corners, generally resembling some petrified monster, frightful and gigantic, on its back with its legs in the air.* OUR MUTUAL FRIEND BOOK ii, CH. I

Circumlocution Office, Whitehall Whitehall is so full of Government offices that we may take any one of them as being the Circumlocution Office to which Arthur Clennam went so often to interview the various members of the Tite Barnacle family. *No public business of any kind could possibly be done at any time, without the acquiescence of the Circumlocution Office ... with wrongs, or with projects for general welfare. Unfortunates ... who ... never reappeared in the light of day.* LITTLE DORRIT BOOK i, CH. X

City Road Little Paul Dombey, in the charge of Polly Toodles and Susan Nipper, was taken from Camden Town to meet the newly made Charitable Grinder – little Biler – in his full charity dress; and about here Florence was stolen by *good Mrs. Brown*. DOMBEY AND SON CH. VI

See Camden Town.

'*My address*', said Mr. Micawber, '*is Windsor Terrace, City Road, I – in short*', said Mr. Micawber, *with the same genteel air, and in another burst of confidence – 'I live there'*. . . . '*Under the impression . . . that you might have some difficulty in penetrating the arcana of the Modern Babylon in the direction of the City Road – in short that you might lose yourself – I shall be happy to call this evening and instal you in the knowledge of the nearest way*.' DAVID COPPERFIELD CH. XI

City Square At the junction of Old Broad Street with Throgmorton Street, there was a small square – reaching not quite to the point made by the junction – that point now covered by a modern bank. In Horwood's Map of 1800, two small squares are to be seen, both with little passages to the outer street, that with the figure 1 on it leading out to Throgmorton Street perhaps the more likely to have been the location of the Cheeryble offices. Brother Charles took Nicholas by the arm and *hurried him along Threadneedle Street, and through some lanes and passages on the right until they, at length, emerged in a quiet shady little square*. NICHOLAS NICKLEBY CH. XXXV, XXXVII

Clapham Rise *The cook (an amiable woman, but of a weak turn of intellect) burst into tears on beholding the kitchen, and requested that her silver watch might be delivered over to her sister (2 Tuppintock's Gardens, Ligg's Walk, Clapham Rise), in the event of anything happening to her from the damp.* (This house has never been traced.) CHRISTMAS STORIES: THE HAUNTED HOUSE

Also in Clapham Rise, at Rose Villa, Mr. Gattleton lived. Here the amateur theatricals took place, thought to be a slice out of Dickens's own life at the age of about twenty-one. SKETCHES BY BOZ: MRS. JOSEPH PORTER; LIFE

Clapham Road The Poor Relation lived in *a very clean back room, in a very respectable house – where I am expected not to be at home in the daytime, unless poorly,* in the Clapham Road. In reality he lived in a castle – in the air! CHRISTMAS STORIES: THE POOR RELATION'S STORY

Clare Market was south of Portsmouth Street. The ancient building 'The Old Curiosity Shop' is the only survival. This building has existed a great many years and in Stuart days was thought to have been a dairy. Dickens is said to have dealt with a bookbinder named Tessyman who carried on his business there. The novelist must certainly have seen the building when calling on his friend John Forster who lived nearby at 58 Lincoln's Inn Fields. At the end of the story of THE OLD CURIOSITY SHOP Dickens says in regard to the home of Little Nell – *The old house had been long ago pulled down.*

The three Maypole cronies, Long Parkes, Tom Cobb and Solomon Daisy *struck through the Forest path upon their way to London; . . . As they drew nearer to their destination, they began to make enquiries of the people whom they passed, concerning the riots.*

Old Curiosity Shop, Clare Market

Among various disturbing reports, one man told them that *the houses of two witnesses near Clare Market were about to be pulled down when he came away.* Little the cronies thought of the destruction they would find at the Maypole and Warren on their return. BARNABY RUDGE CH. LVI

Beresford Chancellor in his book 'The London of Charles Dickens' says that the Sardinia Chapel was burnt by the Gordon Rioters. It stood next to the residence of the

Sardinian Ambassador in Sardinia Street, off Lincoln's Inn Fields.

According to Dickens, *The gin shops . . . in Clare Market* were among *the handsomest in London.* SKETCHES BY BOZ: GIN SHOPS

Clerkenwell *In the venerable suburb – it was a suburb once – of Clerkenwell, towards that part of its confines which is nearest to the Charter House, and in one of those cool, shady streets of which a few . . . yet remain,* lived that honest locksmith, Gabriel Varden, *a modest building, not very straight, not large, not tall; not bold-faced, with great staring windows, but a shy, blinking house, with a conical roof going up into a peak over its garret window of four small panes of glass, like a cocked hat on the head of an elderly gentleman with one eye . . . a great wooden emblem of a key, painted in vivid yellow to resemble gold, which dangled from the house-front, and swung to and fro with a mournful, creaking noise, as if complaining that it had nothing to unlock.* BARNABY RUDGE CH. IV

Prisoners were released from the *New Jail at Clerkenwell* by the Gordon rioters. BARNABY RUDGE CH. LXVI

Mr. Jarvis Lorry *walked along the sunny streets from Clerkenwell, where he lived, on his way to dine with the Doctor* (Dr. Manette, who lived near Soho Square). TALE OF TWO CITIES BOOK ii, CH. VI

Mr. Venus lived *in a narrow and dirty street* in Clerkenwell, at a little dark, greasy shop with a dark window with one tallow candle dimly burning in it, where he was visited by Silas Wegg, who *being on his road to the Roman Empire approaches it by way of Clerkenwell.* He was on his way to read to Mr. Boffin 'The Decline and Fall of the Roman Empire'. OUR MUTUAL FRIEND BOOK i, CH. VII

Clerkenwell Green It was near this Green that Mr. Brownlow, attentively reading a book at a stall outside a shop, was considered *a prime plant,* as the Artful Dodger, Charley Bates and Oliver Twist *were just emerging from a narrow court not far from the open square in Clerkenwell, which is yet called, by some strange perversion of terms 'The Green'.* It was here that Oliver saw to his horror what Fagin's training led to. (The narrow Court is said to be Pear Tree Court.) OLIVER TWIST CH. X

Clerkenwell Sessions House It was to the Clerkenwell Sessions House that Bumble was bound when he announced to Mrs. Mann he was going up to London. *And I very much question whether the Clerkinwell Sessions will not find themselves in the wrong box before they have done with me,* said Mr. Bumble, drawing himself up proudly. OLIVER TWIST CH. XVII

Clifford's Inn, Fleet Street

Cleveland Street Cleveland Street was formerly Green Lanes, where the rioters in BARNABY RUDGE had a meeting place. BARNABY RUDGE CH. XLIV

Clifford's Inn Jack Bamber telling Mr. Pickwick stories of the Inns of Court, in the Magpie and Stump, tells one of a tenant in Clifford's Inn. PICKWICK PAPERS CH. XXI

Tip Dorrit found *a stool and twelve shillings a week* in the office of an attorney in Clifford's Inn and here languished for six months. LITTLE DORRIT BOOK i, CH. VII

Referred to by Trooper George of BLEAK HOUSE as the office of Melchisedeck, the legal agent of old Smallweed. BLEAK HOUSE CH. XXXIV

John Rokesmith made his secretarial proposals to Mr. Boffin in the confines of this Inn. *Would you object to turn aside into this place – I think it is*

*called Clifford's Inn — where we can hear one another better than in
the roaring street?* Mr. Boffin glanced into *the mouldy little
plantation, or cat-preserve, of Clifford's Inn as it was that day. . . .
Sparrows were there, cats were there, dry-rot and wet-rot were there,
but it was not otherwise a suggestive spot.* OUR MUTUAL FRIEND
BOOK i, CH. VIII

The Archway to Clifford's Inn still remains and a
small patch of grass marks the site of the vestry door.
Here the claims for loss in the Great Fire of 1666 were
assessed.

Clifford Street Figures in the paper Dickens wrote on
Arcadian London where he stayed at his hatter's in the dog
days. See Burlington Arcade and Bond Street. UNCOM-
MERCIAL TRAVELLER: ARCADIAN LONDON

Cobley's Farm See Finchley.

Cock Lane (Snow Hill). Mrs. Nickleby in her wandering
way briefly included this with another ghost-ridden spot:
Some of those extraordinary creatures. NICHOLAS NICKLEBY
CH. XLIX

Coleman Street See Bell Alley.

College Street *They met on the appointed night, and, hiring a
hackney coach, directed the driver to stop at the corner of the Old
Pancras Road at which stands the parish workhouse. By the time
they alighted there, it was quite dark; and, proceeding by the dead wall
in front of the Veterinary Hospital, they entered a small by-street,
which is, or was at that time, called Little College Street, and which,
whatever it may be now, was in those days a desolate place enough,
surrounded by little else than fields and ditches.* PICKWICK PAPERS
CH. XXI

Little College Street mentioned above is now College
Place.

Here Dickens lodged for a while after the family left the
Gower Street house and his father and mother were in the
Marshalsea for debt, Mrs. Dickens choosing to join her
husband as a more economical means of living. In his own

words Dickens tells the story: *I was handed over to a reduced old lady, long known to our family, in Little College Street, Camden Town, who took children in to board, and had once done so at Brighton; and who, with a few alterations and embellishments, unconsciously began to sit for Mrs. Pipchin in* DOMBEY AND SON *when she took me in. She had a little brother and sister under her care then; somebody's natural children, who were very irregularly paid for, and a widow's little son. The two boys and I slept in the same room. My own exclusive breakfast of a penny cottage loaf and a pennyworth of milk, I provided for myself. I kept another small loaf, and a quarter of a pound of cheese on a particular shelf of a particular cupboard, to make my supper on when I came back at night. They made a hole in the six or seven shillings, I knew well, and I was out at the blacking warehouse all day and had to support myself on that money all the week. I suppose my lodging was paid for by my father. I certainly did not pay it myself, and I certainly had no other assistance whatever (the making of my clothes, I think, excepted) from Monday morning until Saturday night. No advice, no counsel, no encouragement, no consolation, no support, from anyone that I can call to mind, so help me God.* LIFE; DOMBEY AND SON CH. VIII

College of Surgeons *'That's the thing, sir', repeated Richard, with the greatest enthusiasm. 'We have got it at last. M.R.C.S.' 'By heaven!' cried Mr. Boythorn . . . 'I rejoice to find a young gentleman of spirit and gallantry devoting himself to that noble profession! . . . as for those fellows . . . with pittances too small for the acceptance of clerks, I would have the necks of every one of them wrung, and their skulls arranged in Surgeons' Hall for the contemplation of the whole profession — in order that its younger members might understand from actual measurement in early life, how thick skulls may become!'* BLEAK HOUSE CH. XIII

'They will be a singular party', said Sir John '. . . a very curious party. The hangman himself; the centaur and the madman. The centaur would make a very handsome preparation in Surgeons' Hall and would benefit science extremely. I hope they have taken care to bespeak him'. BARNABY RUDGE CH. LXXV

Commercial Road, Whitechapel. Continuing from Aldgate High Street to Commercial Road, on the right we note that

on a dead wall in the Commercial Road Captain Cuttle bought the
*ballad of considerable antiquity . . . which set forth the courtship and
nuptials of a promising coal-whipper with a certain 'Lovely Peg'.*
DOMBEY AND SON CH. IX

*I had got past Whitechapel Church, and was – rather in-
appropriately for an Uncommercial Traveller – in the Commercial
Road.* UNCOMMERCIAL TRAVELLER: WAPPING WORKHOUSE

Commercial Street, Whitechapel. *On a July morning of this
summer, I walked towards Commercial Street (not Uncommercial
Street, Whitechapel)* writes Dickens. *I had been attracted by the
following handbill printed in rose coloured paper: Self-supporting
Cooking Depot for the Working Classes, Commercial Street,
Whitechapel, where accommodation is provided for dining comfortably
300 persons at a time. Open from 7 a.m. till 7 p.m.* The building
referred to, a house of refreshment no longer, stands at the
corner of Flower and Dean Street, the third street on the
right. Here it was that Dickens sampled the excellent fare
provided at the cost of 4½d, and says *I dined at my Club in Pall
Mall a few days afterwards, for exactly twelve times the money, and
not half so well.* UNCOMMERCIAL TRAVELLER: THE BOILED BEEF
OF NEW ENGLAND

Coram Street This was formerly Great Coram Street and is
described as *somewhere in that partially-explored tract of country
which lies between the British Museum, and a remote village called
Somers Town. The house of Mrs. Tibbs was, decidedly, the neatest
in all Great Coram Street. . . . The wonder was, that the brass doorplate, with the interesting inscription 'Mrs. Tibbs' had never caught
fire from constant friction. There were meat-safe-looking blinds . . .
blue and gold curtains . . . and spring-roller blinds as Mrs. Tibbs
was wont in the pride of her heart to boast 'all the way up'.* SKETCHES
BY BOZ: THE BOARDING HOUSE

Cornhill Bob Cratchit *went down a slide on Cornhill, at the end
of a lane of boys, twenty times in honour of its being Christmas-eve.*
A CHRISTMAS CAROL

Another visitor to Cornhill was Nadgett the mysterious,
who was *first seen every morning coming down Cornhill, so exactly*

like the Nadgett of the day before as to occasion a popular belief that he never went to bed or took his clothes off. He would sit at Garraway's where *he would be occasionally seen drying a very damp pocket-handkerchief before the fire.* MARTIN CHUZZLEWIT CH. XXVIII, XXXVIII

See Garraway's.

The Conduit referred to in the Gordon riots scenes stood at the east end of Cornhill. BARNABY RUDGE CH. I, LXVII

It was when in Cornhill, *near the Royal Exchange*, that Dickens saw the *Cavalcade* – three advertising vans, in one of which when they drew up in Leadenhall Market, he peeped and saw the King of the Bill Stickers. REPRINTED PIECES: BILL STICKING

Covent Garden and Market Covent Garden had a great fascination for Dickens. 'To be taken for a walk . . . especially if it were anywhere about Covent Garden or the Strand, perfectly entranced him with pleasure', says Forster. When living in Bayham Street, he borrowed a copy of George Coleman's 'Broad Grins' which impressed him so much as to Covent Garden that he went down by himself to compare with the book. LIFE

He always started from his rooms here on the Uncommercial Travels. The furnished rooms he rented were at 26 (formerly 11) Wellington Street at the corner of Tavistock Street, where was his office of ALL THE YEAR ROUND. *I can slip out at my door in the small hours after any midnight and in one circuit of the purlieus of Covent Garden Market, can behold a state of infancy and youth, as vile as if a Bourbon sat upon the English throne.* UNCOMMERCIAL TRAVELLER: THE SHORT-TIMERS; THE CITY OF THE ABSENT

Dickens knew *all the regular watermen (for hackney coaches) within three miles of Covent Garden by sight.* SKETCHES BY BOZ: HACKNEY-COACH STANDS.

Covent Garden comes into nearly all Dickens's works. Herbert Pocket went there to get fruit for after dinner. When Pip received Wemmick's warning at the Temple Gate: *Don't go home,* he *got a late hackney chariot and drove to the Hummums* at the corner of Russell Street (now Russell Chambers) in Covent Garden . . . *in those times a bed was always to be got there at any hour of the night . . . it was a sort of vault on the ground floor at the back, with a despotic monster of a four-post bedstead in it, straddling over the whole place, putting one of his arbitrary legs into the fireplace and another into the doorway, and squeezing the wretched little washing stand in quite a Divinely Righteous manner.* GREAT EXPECTATIONS CH. XXI

Tom and Ruth Pinch strolled here. MARTIN CHUZZLEWIT CH. XL

Sikes refers to it as *Common Garden* where fifty boys could be found any night to pick from, so why *take so much pains about one chalk-faced kid?* (Oliver). OLIVER TWIST CH. XIX

David used to stare at the pineapples when a boy; Steerforth told David that he was going *to breakfast with one of those fellows who is at the Piazza Hotel in Covent Garden.* When better off, David got fruit here for his party, as did Herbert Pocket. He bought a bouquet for Dora. Later, David and his aunt had a temporary lodging in Covent Garden after vacating their two cottages at Highgate. Twice David went to the theatre in Covent Garden, probably each time to the Covent Garden Theatre, first to see Julius Caesar and the new pantomime, after his party. The present 'Garden' dates from 1858, the previous one was destroyed by fire two years earlier. DAVID COPPERFIELD CH. XI, XXIV, XXXIII, LV

Covent Garden Market at sunrise, too, in the spring or summer, when the fragrance of sweet flowers is in the air, overpowering even the unwholesome streams of last night's debauchery, and driving the dusky thrush, whose cage has hung outside a garret window all night long, half mad with joy. OLD CURIOSITY SHOP CH. I

After an exciting evening carrying news to Mr. Perker and his clerk which the next day would lead to Mr. Pickwick's release from the Fleet, Job Trotter, having nowhere to go, spent the night in Covent Garden in a vegetable basket. PICKWICK PAPERS CH. XLVII

The drunken father of Jenny Wren *staggered into Covent Garden Market and there bivouacked to have an attack of the trembles succeeded by an attack of the horrors, in the doorway.* OUR MUTUAL FRIEND BOOK iv, CH. IX

The building at the corner of James Street was formerly the Piazza Hotel (known as Cuttris's), where also Dickens stayed in 1844 on coming to London from Italy specially to read THE CHIMES to a select circle of his friends. That he was familiar with the place is shown from a letter he wrote to Forster at the time saying *I shall look for you at the further table by the fire, where we generally go.* LIFE

Covent Garden and Market
about 1970

Covent Garden Market, when it was market morning, was wonderful company. . . . But one of the worst night sights I know in London is to be found in the children who prowl about this place . . . and are perpetually making a blunt pattering on the pavement of the Piazza with the rain of their naked feet. . . . There was early coffee to be got about Covent Garden. . . . Toast of a very substantial quality was likewise procurable. . . . UNCOMMERCIAL TRAVELLER: NIGHT WALKS

South of the Market by St. Paul's Church is Henrietta Street, Covent Garden, where at No. 11 were the publishing offices of Chapman & Hall, the firm so closely associated with Dickens's books. LIFE

Covent Garden Market and the avenues leading to it, are thronged with carts of all sorts, sizes, and descriptions. . . . SKETCHES BY BOZ: THE STREETS — MORNING

There is a fine secrecy and mystery about the Piazza — how you get up to those rooms above it and what reckless deeds are done there. MISCELLANEOUS PAPERS: WHERE WE STOPPED GROWING

Covent Garden Theatre (destroyed by fire 1856, rebuilt 1858). In the days before 'Pickwick', Dickens actually had an appointment with the stage manager which was never kept, because of a severe cold. LIFE

Mr. John Dounce would make one of a party of four choice spirits for a *half price visit to Drury Lane or Covent Garden, to see two acts of a five-act play, or a new farce, perhaps, or a ballet.* SKETCHES BY BOZ: THE MISPLACED ATTACHMENT OF MR. JOHN DOUNCE

Craven Street In lodgings here Mr. Brownlow had the interview with Rose Maylie that resulted in the recovery of Oliver Twist. OLIVER TWIST CH. XLI

On the site now occupied by Charing Cross railway station stood Hungerford Market, where Dickens worked as a boy. *The blacking warehouse was the last house on the left-hand side of the way at Old Hungerford Stairs . . . it was a crazy, tumble-down old house abutting of course on the river, and literally overrun with rats . . . the counting house was on the first floor looking over the coal barges on the river. There was a recess in it, in which I was to sit and work.* LIFE

Crockford's 50 St. James's Street (building now offices). There is a passing reference to this once famous Club, which was closed in 1944, in NICHOLAS NICKLEBY CH. II

Cross Keys Inn, Wood Street. Pip arrived here, from Rochester, having *got into the ravel of traffic frayed out about the Cross Keys, Wood Street, Cheapside, London.* GREAT EXPECTATIONS CH. XX

We stood in the Inn Yard (The Cross Keys) *while she* (Estella) *pointed out her luggage to me . . . I requested a waiter . . . to show us a private sitting room.* Here Pip ordered *some tea for the lady.* The air of the room into which they were shown *might have led one to infer that the coaching department was not doing well, and that the enterprising proprietor was boiling down the horses for the refreshment department . . . yet the room was*

all in all to me, Estella being in it. GREAT EXPECTATIONS CH.
XXXIII

At No. 128 Wood Street stood the Cross Keys Inn, at
which Dickens himself arrived as a boy from Chatham on
the family coming to London. *Through all the years that have
passed since,* he wrote, *have I ever lost the smell of the damp straw
in which I was packed – like game – and forwarded carriage paid
to the Cross Keys, Wood Street, Cheapside, London?* LIFE; UN-
COMMERCIAL TRAVELLER: DULLBOROUGH TOWN

*We have also travelled occasionally, with a small boy of pale
aspect, with light hair, and no perceptible neck, coming up to town
from school under the protection of the guard, and directed to be left
at the Cross Keys till called for.* SKETCHES BY BOZ: OMNIBUSES

Mr. Baptist, a foreigner, is run over and an onlooker
blamed the accident on *them Mails . . . they come a racing out of
Lad Lane and Wood Street at twelve or fourteen mile an hour, them
Mails do. The only wonder is, that people ain't killed oftener by them
Mails.* And another bystander added: *I see one on 'em go over
a cat, sir – and it might have been your own mother.* LITTLE DORRIT
BOOK i, CH. XIII

Crown Inn Standing at the corner of Brewer Street and
Lower James Street, it is possibly a successor to that named
by Newman Noggs, on the corner of Beak Street (formerly
Silver Street) and Upper James Street. NICHOLAS NICKLEBY
CH. VII

Cursitor Street Mr. Skimpole took Mr. Jarndyce, Ada and
Esther Summerson to see what *Coavinses* the sheriff's
officer, had left. Three children. No mother. He took them
to Cursitor Street, Chancery Lane, where there was a house
with barred windows, which he called Coavinses Castle.
Coavinses was Mr. Skimpole's nickname for Neckett.
BLEAK HOUSE CH. XV

Mr. John Dounce *was a retired glove and braces maker, a
widower, resident with three daughters – all grown up, and all
unmarried – in Cursitor Street, Chancery Lane.* SKETCHES BY BOZ:
THE MISPLACED ATTACHMENT OF MR. JOHN DOUNCE

Arrested for debt, Mr. Watkins Tottle was confined in a sponging house in Cursitor Street, Chancery Lane. SKETCHES BY BOZ: PASSAGE IN THE LIFE OF MR. WATKINS TOTTLE

Custom House (Lower Thames Street). The late Mr. Bardell was employed here. PICKWICK PAPERS CH. XXXIV

Peepy also had a position here and was reported to be *doing extremely well.* BLEAK HOUSE CH. LXVII

David, on his return to London from his long tour abroad, after the death of Dora, *landed . . . on a wintry autumn evening* and *walked from the Custom House to the Monument* before he could find a coach to take him to Gray's Inn. DAVID COPPERFIELD CH. LIX

Pip always left his boat *at a wharf near the Custom House, to be brought up afterwards to the Temple Stairs*, part of a scheme to get Magwitch out of the country. GREAT EXPECTATIONS CH. XLVII

Somewhere in this neighbourhood, between the Custom House and London Bridge, Dickens placed Spigwiffin's Wharf, where Ralph Nickleby found house room for Mrs. Nickleby and Kate. Mrs. Nickleby explained that the way to the house was *all down Newgate Street, all down Cheapside, all up Lombard Street, down Gracechurch Street, and along Thames Street, as far as Spigwiffin's Wharf. Oh! it's a mile!* NICHOLAS NICKLEBY CH. XXVI

In the same direction was Mrs. Clennam's house. When Arthur visited it on his return to England *he crossed by St. Paul's and went down at a long angle, almost to the water's edge, through some of the crooked and descending streets which lie, and lay more crookedly and closely then, between the river and Cheapside.* The house he sought was *an old brick house which . . . many years ago . . . had it in its mind to slide down sideways; it had been propped up, however, and was leaning on some half dozen gigantic crutches.* LITTLE DORRIT BOOK i, CH. XXIX

It was at one of the wharves in Thames Street that poor Florence, after having been robbed of her clothes by *good Mrs. Brown*, was discovered by Walter Gay. DOMBEY AND SON CH. VI

And it was Mrs. MacStinger's friend, Mrs. Bokum, whose deceased husband had also been employed in the Custom House. DOMBEY AND SON CH. VI

Cuttris's Hotel See Covent Garden and Market.

Deptford Walter Gay referred to *Private West India Trader, burden three hundred and fifty tons, Captain John Brown of Deptford. Owners, Wiggs & Co.* DOMBEY AND SON CH. IV

Devonshire House Dickens acted here before Queen Victoria in 1851 in Lytton's comedy 'Not So Bad As We Seem', a prelude to some splendid strolling by Dickens and his friends for the noble cause of charity. (Demolished 1924. Berkeley Street and Mayfair Place constructed partly on the site.) LIFE

Devonshire Terrace, No. 1. A corner house where Dickens lived from 1839–1851. It saw the output of many of the most important novels – OLD CURIOSITY SHOP, BARNABY RUDGE, DOMBEY AND SON, DAVID COPPERFIELD, and three of the famous Christmas Books.

In 1962 the house was demolished, the site forming the eastern end of a terrace to be used for offices. The architects have cut an angle out of the building on the site of the house and inserted a large, rectangular, carved mural showing Dickens's head in the centre and a number of his characters particularly concerned with Marylebone, as in DOMBEY AND SON. They have also inserted a large slab over the approximate site of the doorway to No. 1 Devonshire Terrace, which faced Marylebone High Street, on which a part of Dickens's letter to Forster, recording his sadness on leaving this home, is inscribed in gilt lettering.

Doctors' Commons Once the College of the Doctors of Law, who lived together in the collegiate manner for meals and lodging. It was demolished in 1867 to make room for Queen Victoria Street, which passes through the site of the quadrangular garden of the college.

A Telephone Exchange stands on the north part of Doctors' Commons site, Queen Victoria Street on its southern. A long, completely blank wall on the remains of Knightrider Street there marks the northern boundary of this former sanctuary of the law.

The five Courts conducted in Doctors' Commons, the Courts of Arches, Prerogative and Dispensations, the Consistory Court of the Bishop of London and the High Court of Admiralty, passed to the jurisdiction of the Law Courts after they were opened in the Strand in 1882.

Deans Court, on the right at the top of Ludgate Hill, leads to what Mr. Boffin called *Doctor Scommons*. OUR MUTUAL FRIEND BOOK i, CH. VIII

Described by Steerforth as *a lazy old nook near Saint Paul's churchyard . . . a little out-of-the-way place . . . that has an ancient monopoly in suits about people's wills and people's marriages*. Here David went with his Aunt for his initial interview with Mr. Spenlow and here in due course he entered into his role as an articled clerk and eventually, invited to Mr. Spenlow's house, fell in love with Dora. DAVID COPPERFIELD CH. XXIII, XXXIII

Jingle came here for his marriage licence, not deterred by Sam's story concerning proctors at the entrance to the Commons. PICKWICK PAPERS CH. X

Another amusing incident concerning Doctors' Commons occurs in connection with Tony Weller's inheritance from his second wife, married entirely on account of the above mentioned proctors! Having told his son that the will provided for *Two hundred pound vurth o' reduced counsels to my son-in-law Samivel*, the rest to himself, he was about to put it on the fire as done with. Sam, shocked and preventing this, explained *it must be proved, and probated, and swore to, and all manner o' formalities*. A lawyer was engaged, one known to

Tony as *a confidential pal o' the Chancellorships* to whom at the first interview Tony explained, *Wot we rekvire, sir, is a probe o' this here*, producing the will. Various visits to Doctors' Commons resulted till the day came for one to the Stock Exchange, *up a court behind the Bank of England*, when at first Tony insisted on cashing the cheque in payment for the Stock sold, in nothing but *golden sovereigns*. PICKWICK PAPERS CH. LV

Dickens rented an office in 1831 at No. 5 Bell Yard, off Carter Lane, leading also direct into the Commons. In a letter to Forster some years later Dickens told him how nearly he had had a chance to go on the stage. He had been stopped by a cold and *inflammation of the face* and soon after, he had *made a splash in the Gallery* (of the House of Commons). The chance then opening, he had commenced to write – all during his tenancy of No. 5 Bell Yard (gone). LIFE

Very well! said Doyce. *Then if this young lady will do me the honour of regarding me for four and twenty hours in the light of a father, and will take a ride with me now towards St. Paul's churchyard, I dare say I know what we want to get there.* (By implication, a marriage licence.) LITTLE DORRIT BOOK ii, CH. XXXIV

Doughty Street, 'Dingley Dell' Kitchen

The place where they grant marriage-licences to love-sick couples, and divorce to unfaithful ones; register the wills of people who have property to leave, and punish hasty gentlemen who call ladies by unpleasant names. SKETCHES BY BOZ: DOCTORS' COMMONS

Doughty Street, No. 48 Dickens lived here from 1837–39. It was the first home he rented after his marriage and the birth of his first child, having lodged before in Furnival's Inn, which became too cramped for his growing family. Here PICKWICK PAPERS was finished, OLIVER TWIST and NICHOLAS NICKLEBY written and BARNABY RUDGE begun.

The house is now the Headquarters of the Dickens Fellowship and a Museum and Library. LIFE

Dover Road David's flight on foot to Dover and his Aunt Betsey Trotwood began on this road, his box and money having been stolen at the Obelisk by the *long-legged young man* who had driven off. DAVID COPPERFIELD CH. XII

Mr. Peggotty on his first return to London after his search for Little Em'ly, told David as he began his return journey he *knew he could find a clean, plain lodging for the night* on the Dover Road. DAVID COPPERFIELD CH. XL

There's milestones on the Dover Road said Mr. F's Aunt. LITTLE DORRIT BOOK i, CH. XXIII

The story concerned with the French Revolution really begins on the Dover Road and on the Dover Mail, on a filthy night of mud, mist and cold, showing how aware, armed and courageous coach and guard had to be on such journeys. TALE OF TWO CITIES BOOK i, CH. II

Drummond Street Near Euston Station is Drummond Street, where at No. 47 The Mistaken Milliner, Miss Martin, lived. SKETCHES BY BOZ: THE MISTAKEN MILLINER. A TALE OF AMBITION

When at school at the Wellington House Academy, Camden Town, it was in Drummond Street that Charles Dickens, with other boys, asked old ladies for charity as a joke. LIFE

Drury Lane Where Charles Dickens, and David Copperfield, ordered *a small plate of beef*. The exact site of Johnson's alamode beef house is given as Clare Court, according to the portion of autobiography published by Forster in his LIFE OF CHARLES DICKENS. This Court was cleared away in 1905 for the Aldwych improvements; Kean Street, Drury Lane, marks the site.

Dick Swiveller had apartments in the Lane, which, *in addition to this conveniency of situation had the advantage of being over a tobacconist's shop, so that he was enabled to procure a refreshing sneeze at any time by merely stepping out on the staircase, and was saved the trouble and expense of maintaining a snuff box.* OLD CURIOSITY SHOP CH. VII

The pawnbroker's shop is situated near Drury Lane at the corner of a court. SKETCHES BY BOZ: THE PAWNBROKER'S SHOP

A broker's shop is, in effect, one of cheap, second-hand goods, mostly furniture and household items, which somewhat adapts its wares to its neighbourhood. Thus, in Drury Lane everything to do with the theatre is a feature, shoes and boots, finery, swords, gauntlets, portraits, as in anywhere near the river, the shop, then a Marine Store, turns to seafaring garb. SKETCHES BY BOZ: BROKERS' AND MARINE STORE SHOPS

The gin shops in and near Drury Lane, Holborn, St. Giles's, Covent Garden and Clare Market, are the handsomest in London. SKETCHES BY BOZ: GIN SHOPS

Mr. Dumps, on his way to the dreaded Christening, was taken far beyond *Doory Lane*, by the *cad* (conductor), and intended not to pay the fare. On the offer of the driver to take him back *to the Edge-er (Edgware) Road for nothing and set him down at Doory Lane*, he decided to pay the disputed 6*d*. and got off then and there. SKETCHES BY BOZ: BLOOMSBURY CHRISTENING

If you meet a man, lounging up Drury Lane, . . . with his hands in the pockets of a pair of dark trousers plentifully besprinkled with grease-spots . . . don't pity him. He is not shabby-genteel. SKETCHES BY BOZ: SHABBY GENTEEL PEOPLE

Crown Court, beside the Fortune Theatre in Russell Street, on the left of Drury Lane, leads to a playing ground called

Drury Lane Garden, the original Poor Jo's churchyard where Captain Hawdon was buried: *a hemmed-in churchyard, pestiferous and obscene, whence malignant diseases are communicated to the bodies of our dear brothers and sisters who have not departed; while our dear brothers and sisters who hang about official backstairs – would to Heaven they had departed! – are very complacent and agreeable.* BLEAK HOUSE CH. XI

Drury Lane Theatre

Drury Lane Theatre (exterior as rebuilt in 1812). At the corner of Catherine and Russell Streets. Miss Petowker, of the Vincent Crummles Company, was described as *of the Theatre Royal, Drury Lane.* At the Kenwigs' party Miss Henrietta Petowker gave a rendering of The Blood Drinker's Burial. *That young lady let down her back hair . . . and went through the performance with extraordinary spirit and to the great terror of the little Kenwigses.* NICHOLAS NICKLEBY CH. XIV

Mr. Smangle describes Mr. Mivins as a man with *comic powers that would do honour to Drury Lane Theatre.* PICKWICK PAPERS CH. XLIV

The Uncommercial Traveller, after saying: *Those wonderful houses about Drury Lane Theatre, which in the palmy days of theatres were prosperous,* goes on to compare them with his

own day when they *now change hands every week,* showing
every sign of degeneration, but he enlarges on the success
of a cheap theatre which yet manages to be successful.
UNCOMMERCIAL TRAVELLER: TWO VIEWS OF A CHEAP THEATRE

*The proprietor of a private theatre may be an ex-scene painter,
a low coffee house keeper, a disappointed eighth-rate actor, a retired
smuggler, or uncertified bankrupt.
The theatre itself may be in
Catherine Street, Strand* (by implication Drury Lane Theatre),
the purlieus of the City. SKETCHES
BY BOZ: PRIVATE THEATRES

Poll Green, one of Dickens's
companions at the Blacking
Warehouse, *had the additional
distinction of being the son of a fire-
man, who was employed at Drury
Lane Theatre, where another relation
of Poll's, I think his little sister, did
imps in the pantomimes.* LIFE

Duke Street Mr. Twemlow,
the *innocent piece of dinner-
furniture that went upon easy
castors and was kept over a livery
stable-yard, in Duke Street, St.
James's, when not in use.* OUR
MUTUAL FRIEND BOOK i, CH. II

Duke of York's Column
*What would your sabbath en-
thusiasts say, to an aristocratic
ring encircling the Duke of York's*

Duke of York's Column and Steps

Column in Carlton Terrace . . . ? SKETCHES BY BOZ: FIRST OF MAY

Dulwich *The house I have taken,* said Mr. Pickwick, *is at
Dulwich. It has a large garden, and is situated in one of the most
pleasant spots near London.* A house in Dulwich Village claims
to be where Mr. Pickwick retired.

Later in the same chapter we read: *Mr. Pickwick is somewhat infirm now; but he retains all his former juvenility of spirit, and may still be frequently seen, contemplating the pictures in the Dulwich Gallery, or enjoying a walk about the pleasant neighbourhood on a fine day.*
PICKWICK PAPERS CH. LVII

The Eagle On the right of the City Road, going north, after passing Shepherdess Walk, almost at the corner stands a modern public house, the Eagle, on the site of the famous Gardens of that name.
SKETCHES BY BOZ: MISS EVANS AND THE EAGLE

Eel Pie Island Twickenham. The Kenwigs family came here and had *a cold collation of bottled beer, shrub and shrimps.*
NICHOLAS NICKLEBY CH. LII
Dickens came here on river trips whilst living at Twickenham and Petersham. LIFE

Ely Place, Charterhouse Street

Ely Place Agnes Wickfield stayed here with the Waterbrooks and was visited here by David Copperfield. David looked up at the clock on St. Andrew's church. DAVID COPPERFIELD CH. XXV

Essex Street, Strand. Here Pip found *a respectable lodging house in Essex Street* for his 'uncle', Mr. Provis, alias Magwitch, the back of which looked into the Temple and was almost within hail of his own chambers in Garden Court. GREAT EXPECTATIONS CH. XL

Field Lane, Holborn (swept away in building of Holborn Viaduct). *Covered ways and yards, which here and there diverged from the main street ... where drunken men and women were positively wallowing in filth* and where *great ill-looking fellows were cautiously emerging, bound ... on no very well disposed or harmless errands,* so to the door of a house near Field Lane – Fagin's Den. OLIVER TWIST CH. VIII

Finchley Barnaby and his father, after escaping from Newgate, found, in a pasture near Finchley, a poor shed with walls of mud and a roof of grass and brambles, now deserted. Here they lay down for the rest of the night. BARNABY RUDGE CH. LXVIII

Abel Cottage, Finchley, home of Mr. and Mrs. Garland, was where Kit and Barbara were employed. *It was a beautiful little cottage with a thatched roof and little spires at the gable ends, and pieces of stained glass in some of the windows, were almost as large as pocket books.* OLD CURIOSITY SHOP CH. XXII

Mr. Toots refers to *going as far as Finchley to get some uncommonly fine chickweed that grows there,* for Miss Dombey's bird. DOMBEY AND SON CH. XXXII

At Cobley's Farm, Finchley, Dickens took lodgings in 1843 whilst writing a part of MARTIN CHUZZLEWIT. Forster tells us that while walking here 'in the green lanes as the mid-summer months were coming on, his introduction of Mrs. Gamp and the uses to which he should apply that remarkable personage, first occurred to him'. No. 70 Queen's Avenue, Finchley, marks the site of Cobley's Farm, and a tablet on the house connects the spot with Dickens and Mrs. Gamp. LIFE

Fitzroy Street, W1. Dickens lodged here as a youth in 1830–33 at No. 15, now No. 25. LIFE

Fleet prison was on the site later occupied by the Memorial Hall, Farringdon Street. Here Mr. Pickwick was imprisoned for refusing to pay the costs and damages awarded Mrs. Bardell in the Breach of Promise case. PICKWICK PAPERS CH. XL, XLIII

The Fleet was one of the prisons on which notices were affixed announcing that the rioters would come that night to burn them down. BARNABY RUDGE CH. LXVII

Fleet Street In Fleet Street, Mr. Boffin was addressed by John Rokesmith, a stranger. Rokesmith offered his services as secretary, and later was engaged in this capacity. OUR MUTUAL FRIEND BOOK i, CH. VIII

In his days of poverty, between eleven and twelve years old, when he had no money to buy food, David Copperfield used to look at a pastry or venison shop in Fleet Street. DAVID COPPERFIELD CH. XI

David, en route with his Aunt for Doctors' Commons to investigate his chance of entering on the life of a Proctor *made a pause at a toy-shop in Fleet Street to see the giants of Saint Dunstan's strike upon the bells – we had timed our going, so as to catch them at it at twelve o'clock.* DAVID COPPERFIELD CH. XXIII

Again David Copperfield having taken the management of Peggotty's affairs into his own hands proved the will and came to a settlement with the Legacy Duty Office. *We varied the legal character of these proceedings by going to see some perspiring Wax Works in Fleet Street.* (Mrs. Salmon's Wax Works at No. 17 Fleet Street.) DAVID COPPERFIELD CH. XXXIII

Folly Ditch *Near to that part of the Thames on which the church at Rotherhithe abuts . . . stands Jacob's Island, surrounded by a muddy ditch, six or eight feet deep and fifteen or twenty wide when the tide is in, once called Mill Pond, but known in the days of this story as Folly Ditch.* OLIVER TWIST CH. L

Foster Lane *A dim, dirty, smoky, tumble-down, rotten old house it was as anybody would desire to see.* No. 5 Foster Lane (Priest's Court) is pointed out as very likely premises for the Chuzzlewits, father and son, having a side entrance which was found so useful by Jonas when planning the alibi for his murder of Montague Tigg. MARTIN CHUZZLEWIT CH. XI

Foundling Hospital Tattycorum in LITTLE DORRIT came from the Foundling Hospital and the story of NO THOROUGH-FARE opens there with a very dramatic scene in which the mother prevails upon one of the servants to point out her son.

Fox-under-the-Hill See Adelphi.

Freeman's Court The open space on the east end of the Royal Exchange, rebuilt since Pickwick's time, covers the ground once occupied by Freeman's Court. Dodson and Fogg had their offices *in the ground floor of a dingy house, at the very furthest end of Freeman's Court, Cornhill . . .* the clerks *catching as favourable glimpses of Heaven's light and Heaven's sun . . . as a man might hope to do were he placed at the bottom of a reasonably deep well; and without the opportunity of perceiving tho stars in the daytime, which the latter secluded situation affords.* PICKWICK PAPERS CH. XX

Freemason's Tavern, Great Queen Street. *Let us suppose you are induced to attend a dinner* on behalf of the 'Indigent Orphans' Friends' Benevolent Institution' at the *Freemason's, round which a crowd of people are assembled* and hear the speculation among them *of your being the noble Lord who is announced to fill the chair on the occasion, and are highly gratified to hear it*

eventually decided that you are only a 'wocalist'. SKETCHES BY BOZ:
PUBLIC DINNERS

This tavern was the scene of a farewell dinner given to
Dickens in 1867, on the eve of his departure to America,
when Lord Lytton was in the chair. The tavern is now
rebuilt. LIFE

Fresh Wharf On the City side of London Bridge. Mrs.
Gamp, enquiring for *The Ankworks package,* wished it was
in Jonadge's belly. She was on the wharf with the idea of
looking out for Mercy Pecksniff, now Mrs. Jonas Chuzzlewit.
MARTIN CHUZZLEWIT CH. XL

An amusing scene of confusion is described by Dickens.
An officer of St. Katherine's Dock Company, stoutly
defending its reputation for protecting *life and property,* says
*if it had been the London Bridge Wharf Company . . . he shouldn't
have wondered, seeing that the morality of that Company* (they
being the opposition) *can't be answered for, by no one,* asserting
the gentleman'll find his luggage afore he gets to Margate. SKETCHES
BY BOZ: THE RIVER

Furnival's Inn, Holborn. The Prudential Assurance Company office covers the site of this Inn, where Dickens had
chambers from 1834 until 1837 when he moved with his
young wife and their first child to No. 48 Doughty Street,
WC1, a short walk away. Here PICKWICK PAPERS was
commenced, from the success of which, after the first few
chapters, Dickens never looked back. LIFE

John Westlock had rooms here. *There is little enough to see
in Furnival's Inn. It is a shady, quiet place, echoing the footsteps of
the stragglers who have business there; and rather monotonous and
gloomy on summer evenings.* MARTIN CHUZZLEWIT CH. XXXVI,
XXXVII, XLV, LIII

The hotel in the Inn (Wood's) was patronised by Mr.
Grewgious for meals and from here to Staple Inn dashed
the *flying waiter.* Here Mr. Grewgious found accommodation
for Rosa Budd. EDWIN DROOD CH. XI, XX

Furnival Street See Castle Street.

Garraway's, a famous City coffee house, stood until 1874 in Change Alley, the third turning on the right in Cornhill, going citywards, where a plaque commemorates the fact. It was from Garraway's that Mr. Pickwick indited his famous *chops and tomato sauce* epistle to Mrs. Bardell. PICKWICK PAPERS CH. XXXIV

Nadgett, the enquiry agent, would sit at Garraway's where he would be *occasionally seen drying a very damp pocket handkerchief before the fire.* MARTIN CHUZZLEWIT CH. XXVII

The Poor Relation used to tell the assembled family that he went into the City every day – he didn't know why – and sat in Garraway's Coffee House. CHRISTMAS STORIES: THE POOR RELATION'S STORY

Mr. Flintwich was a regular customer here, too. LITTLE DORRIT BOOK i, CH. XXIX

The Uncommercial writes of the City Courts on a Sunday: *And here is Garraway's, bolted and shuttered hard and fast! It is possible to imagine the man who cuts the sandwiches, on his back in a hayfield . . . but imagination is unable to pursue the men who wait at Garraway's all the week for the men who never come. When they are forcibly put out of Garraway's on a Saturday night – which they must be . . . where do they vanish until Monday morning?* UNCOMMERCIAL TRAVELLER: THE CITY OF THE ABSENT

See Cornhill.

George Inn See Borough.

George Yard, Lombard Street. Here is the George and Vulture Inn. And here Mr. Pickwick and Sam took up their abode in very good, old fashioned and comfortable quarters after leaving Mrs. Bardell's in Goswell Street. Here the Pickwickians were served with subpoenas in the famous action for Breach of Promise, and from here in due course they all went to the trial at Guildhall. PICKWICK PAPERS CH. XXVI, XXX

Asked by Mr. Bob Sawyer: *I say, old boy, where do you hang out?* Mr. Pickwick replied *that he was at present suspended at the George and Vulture.* PICKWICK PAPERS CH. XXX

Gerrard Street At No. 10, Dickens's uncle, Thomas Barrow, lived in the upper part of the house of a bookseller named Manson. Here Dickens had access to an array of books and was, for some time, supremely happy. LIFE

In that same street – possibly the same house – lived Mr. Jaggers, the lawyer in GREAT EXPECTATIONS. It was *rather a stately house of its kind, but dolefully in want of painting and with dirty windows.* GREAT EXPECTATIONS CH. XXVI

Golden Cross Hotel See Charing Cross.

George and Vulture Inn

Golden Dog Licking Pot Crossing Blackfriars Bridge, Union Street was to be found on the left with the Golden Dog licking a golden pot over a shop door on the right corner, a memory of Dickens's boyhood and the Blacking factory. This tradesman's sign is now in the Cuming Museum, Walworth. LIFE

Golden Square In the part of London *in which Golden Square is situated there is a by-gone, faded, tumbledown street, with two irregular rows of tall, meagre houses.* In this neighbourhood the Kenwigs family lived and Newman Noggs and Nicholas Nickleby had lodgings. NICHOLAS NICKLEBY CH. XIV

In a street of this kind, David Copperfield, assisted by Martha, found Little Em'ly. *They alighted at one of the entrances to the Square and hurried to one of the streets of which there are several in that part where the houses were once fair dwellings.* DAVID COPPERFIELD CH. L

Ralph Nickleby lived *in a spacious house in Golden Square, which, in addition to a brass plate upon the street-door, had another brass plate, two sizes and a half smaller upon the left-hand door-post . . . displaying the word 'Office'; it was clear that Mr. Ralph Nickleby did, or pretended to do, business of some kind.* No. 7 (now demolished) was the most likely house and was once that of William à Beckett, with whom Dickens was acquainted. NICHOLAS NICKLEBY CH. II

Goswell Road (Street in Dickens's time). *Mr. Samuel Pickwick . . . threw open his chamber window, and looked out upon the world beneath. Goswell Street was at his feet, Goswell Street was on his right hand – as far as the eye could reach, Goswell Street extended on his left; and the opposite side of Goswell Street was over the way.* PICKWICK PAPERS CH. II, XII, XXXIV

Gower Street (North in Dickens's day). On the site of Maple's premises formerly stood No. 4 Gower Street North, where the Dickens family lived for a short time in 1824, and where Mrs. Dickens tried to start a school for young ladies, as did Mrs. Micawber in DAVID COPPERFIELD. LIFE; DAVID COPPERFIELD CH. XI

Gray's Inn The *old woman* who opened the door to Mr. Pickwick and Sam, called herself Mr. Perker's *laundress*, which gave rise to Mr. Pickwick's remark *'it's a curious circumstance, Sam, that they call the old women in these Inns laundresses. I wonder what that's for?' ' Cos they has a mortal awersion to washing anything, I suppose, sir'*, replied Mr. *Weller.* PICKWICK PAPERS CH. XX

Gray's Inn, gentlemen. Curious little nooks in a great place like London, these old Inns are. PICKWICK PAPERS CH. XX

Job Trotter ran from the Fleet Prison to the gate of Gray's Inn. PICKWICK PAPERS CH. XLVII

Gray's Inn has a great attraction and belies the later description given of it in the UNCOMMERCIAL TRAVELLER as *one of the most depressing institutions in brick and mortar known to the children of men. . . . Sahara desert of the law . . . bills To Let, To Let . . . like gravestones.* UNCOMMERCIAL TRAVELLER: CHAMBERS

Gray's Inn Coffee House On the left of Gray's Inn Gateway is the site of the Gray's Inn Coffee House, at which David Copperfield stayed when visiting Traddles at his Chambers. DAVID COPPERFIELD CH. LIX

Gray's Inn Gardens Flora, in her second wooing of Arthur Clennam, *considered nothing so improbable as that he ever walked on the north-west side of Gray's Inn Gardens at exactly four o'clock in the afternoon.* LITTLE DORRIT BOOK i, CH. XIII

Gray's Inn Hall *Clerk after clerk hastened into the Square by one or other of the entrances, and looking up at the Hall clock, accelerated or decreased his rate of walking according to the time at which his office hours nominally commenced.* PICKWICK PAPERS CH. LIII

Holborn Gate of Gray's Inn

Gray's Inn Lane (now Gray's Inn Road). The place of residence of Mr. Mortimer (otherwise Wilkins Micawber). DAVID COPPERFIELD CH. XXXVI

The patriarchal humbug Casby *lived in a street in the Gray's Inn Road, which had set off from that thoroughfare with the intention of running at one heat down into the valley, and up again to the top of Pentonville Hill; but which had run itself out of breath in twenty yards and had stood still ever since.* LITTLE DORRIT BOOK i, CH. XIII

Dickens adds *there is no such place in that part now*, which was quite true, as the streets had meanwhile been completed; but investigation has shown that Acton Street was for many years only partially built, so it is reasonable to suppose that Acton Street was in his mind when he referred to the street that stopped short.

. . . there never was a more popular dancing academy than *Signor Billsmethi's of the King's Theatre.* It was situated *in the populous and improving neighbourhood of Gray's Inn Lane.* SKETCHES BY BOZ: THE DANCING ACADEMY

See also Smithfield.

Gray's Inn Square Anxious to consult Mr. Perker on behalf of the newly-wed Nathaniel and Arabella and further prompted to come to a pecuniary settlement with the kind-hearted little attorney, Mr. Pickwick made a hurried breakfast and hastened to his Chambers in Gray's Inn Square. PICKWICK PAPERS CH. LIII

Gray's Inn: South Square (formerly Holborn Court). Here Mr. Phunky had Chambers: *Phunky's – Holborn Court, Gray's Inn.* PICKWICK PAPERS CH. XXXI

Traddles's address was Holborn Court (No. 2) where he occupied a set of Chambers on a top storey. When David visited him he had to ascend *a crazy old staircase. I found it feebly lighted on each landing by a club-headed little oil wick, dying away in a little dungeon of dirty glass.* DAVID COPPERFIELD CH. LIX

Dickens was office boy at No. 1 South Square with Ellis and Blackmore before they moved to Raymond Buildings. LIFE

Great Marlborough Street The famous police court here is said to be the one to which Inspector Bucket conducted Esther before commencing his search for Lady Dedlock. BLEAK HOUSE CH. LVII

Mr. Percy Noakes *sallied forth for Mrs. Taunton's domicile in Great Marlborough Street.* SKETCHES BY BOZ: THE STEAM EXCURSION

Great Ormond Street and Hospital Before writing OUR MUTUAL FRIEND Dickens had taken a personal interest in this Hospital and in 1858 took the Chair at a dinner held on its behalf at which he made an eloquent appeal for funds. Forster recorded the incident in full. The sum of £3,000 was raised that night. Shortly after, Dickens gave a reading of A CHRISTMAS CAROL on its behalf, the great success of which led him to commence the Public Readings he gave so successfully. LIFE

Little Johnny died with a kiss for the *Boofer lady* here. OUR MUTUAL FRIEND BOOK ii, CH. IX

Now that the Government was using the extreme prerogative of the Crown to quell the Gordon riots, parties of soldiers were posted before daylight at the Lord Chancellor's in Great Ormond Street, among a number of other important and threatened places. BARNABY RUDGE CH. LXVII

Great Portland Street *Mrs. Briggs was a widow, with three daughters and two sons. . . . They resided in Portland Street, Oxford Street, and moved in the same orbit as the Tauntons – hence their mutual dislike.* SKETCHES BY BOZ: THE STEAM EXCURSION

Great Queen Street, WC2. Dick Swiveller told Fred Trent *I bought a pair of boots in Great Queen Street last week, and made that no thoroughfare, too.* OLD CURIOSITY SHOP CH. VIII

See Freemason's Tavern.

Great Russell Street Mr. Charles Kitterbell lived here at No. 14 (marked by plaque) but *Uncle Dumps always dropped the 'Bedford Square' and inserted in lieu thereof, the dreadful words 'Tottenham Court Road'.* SKETCHES BY BOZ: THE BLOOMSBURY CHRISTENING

At the pipe shop in Great Russell Street, the Death's-head pipers were like theatrical memento mori, admonishing beholders of the decline of the playhouse as an Institution. UNCOMMERCIAL TRAVELLER: TWO VIEWS OF A CHEAP THEATRE

Great Tower Street Joe Willet, having parted with The Maypole, his father and his father's cronies, and having walked to the City, met a Recruiting Sergeant at the Black Lion and hearing him describe military life to half a dozen fellows in the tap room, decided that this was the life for him. Hearing the Sergeant's quarters would be at the Crooked Billet in Tower Street, Joe first paid a fruitless visit to the Vardens' house in the vain hope of some understanding with pretty Dolly, found the Crooked Billet and enlisted for a soldier. BARNABY RUDGE CH. XXXI

In his Church rambles, the Uncommercial noticed the scents and smells peculiar to certain churches and neighbourhoods, as: *From Rood Lane to Tower Street, and thereabouts, there was often a subtle flavour of wine; sometimes, of tea. One church near Mincing Lane smelt like a druggist's drawer.* UNCOMMERCIAL TRAVELLER: CITY OF LONDON CHURCHES; THE DICKENSIAN, SPRING 1948

Green Park The pavement artist in SOMEBODY'S LUGGAGE did not want his loved one to go by Piccadilly, so shy was he of his work which was to be found on the *fine, broad, eligible piece of pavement* by the railings of Green Park. CHRISTMAS STORIES: SOMEBODY'S LUGGAGE

Greenwich At Greenwich Church, Bella was married to John Rokesmith; or, as Dickens puts it, *the church porch, having swallowed up Bella Wilfer for ever and ever, had it not in its power to relinquish that young woman but slid into the happy sunlight Mrs. John Rokesmith instead.* OUR MUTUAL FRIEND BOOK iv, CH. IV

After the wedding, at the Ship Hotel, *The marriage dinner was the crowning success, for what had bride and bridegroom plotted to do, but to have and to hold that dinner in the very room of the hotel where Pa and the lovely woman had once dined together!* . . . *the dishes being seasoned with Bliss — an article which they are sometimes out of at Greenwich.* OUR MUTUAL FRIEND BOOK iv, CH. IV

The Ship Hotel was the scene of that occasion when Bella commanded Pa to *take this lovely woman out to dinner.* . . . *The little room overlooking the river into which they were shown for dinner was delightful. Everything was delightful . . . as they sat looking at the ships and steamboats making their way to the sea with the tide that was running down, the lovely woman imagined all sorts of voyages for herself and Pa.* OUR MUTUAL FRIEND BOOK ii, CH. VIII

Of their many domestic trials, or *ordeal of servants*, as David puts it, the last was *a young person of genteel appearance, who went to Greenwich Fair in Dora's bonnet.* DAVID COPPERFIELD CH. XLIV

Boz says: *In our earlier days we were a constant frequenter of Greenwich Fair, for years.* SKETCHES BY BOZ: GREENWICH FAIR See Blackheath.

Grocers Hall Court On the right going from the Bank along Cheapside, this Court is said to be the place to which Sam Weller, whose *knowledge of London was extensive and peculiar*, directed the steps of Mr. Pickwick for *a glass of brandy and water warm.*

His directions were *Second Court on the right-hand side – last house but vun on the same side of the vay – take the box as stands in the first fireplace, 'cos there ain't no leg in the middle o' the table, vich all the others has.* PICKWICK PAPERS CH. XX

Authorities differ. A claim could be made for Blossoms Inn, in Lawrence Lane, still further west, known to have had a coaching yard.

Grosvenor Square Mr. Tite Barnacle resided here at No. 24, Mews Street, Grosvenor Square, *a hideous little street of dead wall, stables, and dunghills, with lofts over coach-houses inhabited by coachmen's families, who had a passion for drying clothes, and decorating their window-sills with miniature turnpike-gates. . . . To the sense of smell, the house was like a sort of bottle filled with a strong distillation of mews; and when the footman opened the door, he seemed to take the stopper out.* LITTLE DORRIT BOOK i, CH. X

Parties of soldiers were distributed . . . in several private houses (among them, Lord Rockingham's in Grosvenor Square) *which were blockaded* (against the Gordon rioters) *as though to sustain a siege, and had guns pointed from the windows.* BARNABY RUDGE CH. LXVII

We felt certain . . . that he (a little sweep) *would one day be owned by a lord; and we never heard the church-bells ring, or saw a flag hoisted in the neighbourhood, without thinking that the happy event had at last occurred, and that his long lost parent had arrived in a coach-and-six, to take him home to Grosvenor Square.* SKETCHES BY BOZ: FIRST OF MAY

(This illustrated the commonly held belief that sweeps would steal very small boys for the purpose of their trade – to send them up the chimneys – from rich as well as from poor families.)

Guildhall Here the four Pickwickians drove for the famous trial of Bardell *v.* Pickwick. The Guildhall Court has been rebuilt since those days. PICKWICK PAPERS CH. XXXIV

I made up my little mind to seek my fortune . . . my plans . . . were, first to go and see the Giants in Guildhall . . . I found it a long ourney to the Giants and a slow one. . . . Being very tired I got into a corner under Magog, to be out of the way of his eye, and fell asleep. MISCELLANEOUS PAPERS: GONE ASTRAY

Gog and Magog, Guildhall

The following is a description of the City Giants, as seen by Jo Toddyhigh: *The statues of the two Giants, Gog and Magog, each above fourteen feet in height, those which succeeded to still older and more barbarous figures after the Great Fire of London, and which stand in the Guildhall to this day, were endowed with life and motion. These guardian genii of the City had quitted their pedestals, and reclined in easy attitudes in the great stained glass window. Between them was an ancient cask, which seemed to be full of wine; for the younger Giant, clapping his huge hand upon it, and throwing up his mighty leg, burst into an exulting laugh, which reverberated through the hall like thunder.* MASTER HUMPHREY'S CLOCK

Guy's Hospital Bob Sawyer was a medical student at Guy's, *a carver and cutter of live people's bodies* as Mrs. Raddle called him. PICKWICK PAPERS CH. XXXII

There's my lodgings said Mr. Bob Sawyer producing a card, *Lant Street, Borough; it's near Guy's and handy for me, you know ... come on Thursday fortnight, and bring the other chaps with you ... I'm going to have a few medical fellows that night.* Mr. Pickwick expressed the pleasure it would afford him to meet the medical fellows. Mr. Bob Sawyer mentioned that his friend Ben (Allen) was to be one of the party. PICKWICK PAPERS CH. XXX

For Lant Street see Borough.

When Gamp was summoned to his long home, and I see him a-lying in Guy's hospital with a penny-piece on each eye, and his wooden leg under his left arm, I thought I should have fainted away, but I bore up, said Mrs. Gamp. MARTIN CHUZZLEWIT CH. XIX

Ham House The duel between Sir Mulberry Hawk and Lord Frederick Verisopht was fought in one of the fields on the river side of Ham House. The old elm trees along the avenue from the gate at Petersham have been replanted. NICHOLAS NICKLEBY CH. L

Hammersmith Pip, with Herbert Pocket for guide, went by coach to Hammersmith, and after a little walk, lifted the latch of the gate to Mr. Pocket's house, passing direct into a little garden overlooking the river, where the children were playing. He soon observed they were not growing or being brought up, but were tumbling up, seven of them, notwithstanding the two nursemaids in attendance.

The house was run in an inconsequential way owing to Mrs. Pocket's incompetence, but thanks to the servants, the home was a comfortable one, and Pip's room was all he could have desired. Despite a certain vacant air, Mr. Matthew Pocket was an excellent tutor, whom he came to respect and heartily like. GREAT EXPECTATIONS CH. XXII

Clara Barley was met by Herbert Pocket *when she was completing her education at an establishment in Hammersmith.* GREAT EXPECTATIONS CH. XLVI

Mrs. Nickleby tells Kate how *your dear papa's cousin's sister-in-law – a Miss Browndock – was taken into partnership by a lady that kept a school at Hammersmith, and made her fortune in no time at all.* NICHOLAS NICKLEBY CH. XVII

There was a *Miss Maggigg's boarding establishment at Hammersmith* mentioned in MISCELLANEOUS PAPERS: GONE TO THE DOGS

Minerva House, Hammersmith, was a *finishing establishment for young ladies, where some twenty girls of the ages of from thirteen to nineteen inclusive acquired a smattering of everything, and a knowledge of nothing.* SKETCHES BY BOZ: SENTIMENT

Hampstead David Copperfield often took a walk to Hampstead and Highgate after a dip in the Roman Bath in the Strand. DAVID COPPERFIELD CH. XXXV

Dick Swiveller, when he married, lived *in a little cottage at Hampstead . . . which had in its garden a smoking-box, the envy of the civilised world,* and here he was visited by Mr. Chuckster who became *the great purveyor of general news.* OLD CURIOSITY SHOP CH. LXXIII

Speculations on the Source of the Hampstead Ponds was the subject of one of the papers communicated to the Club by Mr. Pickwick. PICKWICK PAPERS CH. I

Jack Straw's Castle (now rebuilt) was a very popular rendezvous with Dickens. Forster quotes the following typical letter from Dickens suggestive of a walk and dinner at this hostelry: *You don't feel disposed, do you, to muffle yourself up and start off with me for a good brisk walk over Hampstead Heath? . . . I know a good 'ouse there where we can have a red hot chop for dinner, and a glass of good wine.* This, Forster adds, *led to our first experience of Jack Straw's Castle, memorable for many happy meetings in coming years.* LIFE

During the writing of PICKWICK PAPERS after the death

of his sister-in-law, Mary Hogarth, Dickens went for a few months to live at Hampstead at Wyldes Farm near the North End. LIFE

The Gordon rioters marched on to Lord Mansfield's country seat at Caen Wood, now Kenwood, between

Wyldes Farm, Hampstead

Hampstead and Highgate, *bent upon destroying that house likewise, and lighting up a great fire there, which from that height should be seen all over London. But in this, they were disappointed, for a party of horse having arrived before them they retreated faster than they went, and came straight back to town.* BARNABY RUDGE CH. LXVI

On his flight after the murder of Nancy, Bill Sikes *skirted Caen Wood and so came out on Hampstead Heath. Traversing the hollow by the Vale of Health, he mounted the opposite bank, and crossing the road which joins the villages of Hampstead and Highgate, made along the remaining portion of the heath to the fields at North End.* OLIVER TWIST CH. XLVIII

Hampstead Road At the corner of Granby Street was the house at which Dickens went to school after his father had come out of the Marshalsea Prison. It was called Wellington House Academy, possibly the original of Mr. Creakle's Salem House Academy in DAVID COPPERFIELD. Dickens wrote that he *went as day scholar to Mr. Jones's establishment which was in Mornington Place.* Dickens writes about this school: *We went to look at it only this last Midsummer and found that the Railway had cut it up, root and branch. A great trunk-line had swallowed the playground, sliced away the schoolroom, and pared off the corner of the house: which, thus curtailed of its proportions, presented itself, in a green stage of stucco, profile-wise towards the road, like a forlorn flat-iron without a handle, standing on end.* (The house has now been demolished.) LIFE; REPRINTED PIECES: OUR SCHOOL; THE DICKENSIAN, AUTUMN 1960

Hanging Sword Alley In Whitefriars Street is Hanging-Sword Alley where Jerry Cruncher lived with his better half, addicted to 'flopping'. *Mr. Cruncher's apartments were not in a savoury neighbourhood, and were but two in number, even if a closet with a single pane of glass in it might be counted as one.* TALE OF TWO CITIES BOOK ii, CH. I

Mr. George walked from his Shooting Gallery near Leicester Square to the Bagnets at Blackfriars through *the cloisterly Temple, and by Whitefriars (there, not without a glance at Hanging-Sword Alley, which would seem to be something in his way).* BLEAK HOUSE CH. XXVII

Hanover Square Thoughts of Sir Mulberry Hawk caused Mrs. Nickleby to think of Kate's marriage *with great splendour at St. George's, Hanover Square.* NICHOLAS NICKLEBY CH. XXI

In reference to 'The Square' (City Square) *in which the counting house of the brothers Cheeryble was situated,* Dickens goes on to say that although *it might not wholly realise the very sanguine expectations which a stranger would be disposed to form on hearing the fervent ecomiums bestowed upon it by Tim Linkinwater,* it was, nevertheless *a sufficiently desirable nook in the heart of a busy town like London. . . . And let not those Londoners whose eyes have been accustomed to the aristocratic gravity of . . . Hanover Square . . . suppose that such feelings had been awakened . . . by any refreshing associations with leaves, however dingy, or grass, however bare and thin.* NICHOLAS NICKLEBY CH. XXXVII

It was at the Hanover Square rooms (on the site of No. 4) that Dickens and his friends gave several presentations of 'Not So Bad As We Seem' and where he gave some of his Public Readings later on. LIFE

In Tenterden Street stood the Royal Academy of Music, which had a personal association with Dickens. As a boy of twelve he was living in Camden Town, his parents in the Marshalsea. His sister Fanny was a student at the Academy, and he tells us that *Sundays, Fanny and I passed in the prison. I was at the Academy, in Tenterden Street, Hanover Square, at nine o'clock in the morning, to fetch her: and we walked back there together at night.* LIFE

Harley Street '*Now Amy*', *said her sister, 'come with me, if you are not too tired to walk to Harley Street, Cavendish Square'. The air with which she threw off this distinguished address, and the toss she gave her new bonnet (which was more gaudy than serviceable) made her sister wonder. . . . Arrived at that grand destination, Fanny singled out the handsomest house, and knocking at the door, inquired for Mrs. Merdle.* LITTLE DORRIT BOOK i, CH. XX

Like unexceptional society, the opposing rows of houses in Harley Street were very grim with one another. Indeed, the mansions and their inhabitants were so much alike in that respect, that the people were often to be found drawn up on opposite sides of dinner-tables, in the shade of their own loftiness, staring at the other side of the way with the dulness of the houses. LITTLE DORRIT BOOK i, CH. XXI

The Uncommercial, noting the peculiarity of the Klem (caretaker) species, says: *This I have discovered in the course of solitary rambles I have taken Northward from my retirement, along the awful perspectives of Wimpole Street, Harley Street, and similar frowning regions,* that is, that they had no idea of the names of the owners, or temporary lodgers, in any of the houses for which they did caretaking, but referred to them as *my good gentleman.* UNCOMMERCIAL TRAVELLER: ARCADIAN LONDON

Hatton Garden At No. 54, the *very notorious Metropolitan Police Office* was presided over by Mr. Fang, according to OLIVER TWIST. In reality it was the Hatton Garden Police Court and a Mr. A. S. Laing was one of the magistrates there between 1836–38. Oliver was brought here *down a place called Mutton Hill where he was led beneath a low archway* *and up a dirty court into this dispensary of summary justice, by the back way.* OLIVER TWIST CH. XI

This way, too, came Nancy, at the request of Fagin, tapping at all the doors with her keys in the endeavour to trace Oliver. OLIVER TWIST CH. XIII

The backs of the houses have now been built over. No. 54 itself is the original building, newly faced over.

The Jellybys once lived in furnished lodgings in Hatton Garden. BLEAK HOUSE CH. XXX

Haymarket The devoted son, Prince, of the selfish old fraud Turveydrop, urged his father to *dine out comfortably somewhere,* to which the reply was *My dear child, I intend to. I shall take my little meal, I think, at the French house, in the Opera Colonnade.* BLEAK HOUSE CH. XIV

The Opera Colonnade was also mentioned in NICHOLAS NICKLEBY CH. II

The reference to the Haymarket and Leicester Square is made to indicate the whereabouts of Mr. George's Shooting Gallery. BLEAK HOUSE CH. XXI

Having spent a certain term abroad at the expense of the British Government, and returned, Mr. Barker officiated as assistant waterman to the hackney coach stand at the corner of the Haymarket, *seated . . . on a couple of tubs near the curb stone. The appearance of the first omnibus caused the public mind to go in a new direction, and prevented a great many hackney coaches from going in any direction at all.* There follows an amusing description, as well as interesting historically, of the rapid development of this kind of public transport, together with Mr. Barker's ingenious way of causing havoc among such passengers – out of sheer spite. SKETCHES BY BOZ: THE LAST CAB-DRIVER AND THE FIRST OMNIBUS CAD

Except in the Haymarket which is the worst kept part of London . . . the peace was seldom violently broken. UNCOMMERCIAL TRAVELLER: NIGHT WALKS

Highgate and Highgate Archway Through Highgate Archway, the one that was replaced by the present one, Noah Claypole and Charlotte came. OLIVER TWIST CH. XLII

The coach rattled along *for Highgate Archway over the hardest ground I have ever heard the ring of iron shoes on.* CHRISTMAS STORIES: HOLLY TREE INN

It was *at the archway toll over at Highgate* that Bucket first picked up the trail of Lady Dedlock. BLEAK HOUSE CH. LVII

Highgate is mentioned as the scene of some of the *unwearied researches* of Mr. Pickwick. PICKWICK PAPERS CH. I

Highgate Church and Cemetery

In South Grove, Highgate, is Church House, said to be the house of Mrs. Steerforth. *An old brick house at Highgate on the summit of the hill ... a genteel, old-fashioned house, very quiet and orderly.* DAVID COPPERFIELD CH. XX

Dr. Strong, after leaving Canterbury, took a cottage here. *It was not in that part of Highgate where Mrs. Steerforth lived, but quite on the opposite side of the little town.*

On his way to visit his old schoolmaster, David went into a cottage that was to let. *It would do for me and Dora admirably: with a little front garden for Jip to run about in ... and a capital room upstairs for my aunt.* DAVID COPPERFIELD CH. XXXVI

To this cottage, David brings his young bride, and later still, while Dora, nursed by Aunt Betsey, is slowly getting weaker, Mr. Peggotty comes to see David, and to him and his Aunt tells Little Em'ly's story, and now that he has her back, their future plans – to emigrate to Australia. From here, David himself is to go abroad one day, having lost his 'child wife'. David's aunt lives in a tiny cottage nearby. DAVID COPPERFIELD CH. XLIII, XLIV, XLVII, LI, LIII

Highgate Church and Cemetery Of St. Michael's Church in South Grove, David writes, *The church with the slender spire,* *that stands on the top of a hill now, was not there then to tell me the time. An old red brick mansion, used as a school, was in its place.* DAVID COPPERFIELD CH. XXXVI

Dickens's father and mother are both buried in Highgate Cemetery, where also lies his little daughter, Dora Annie; two names very reminiscent of two characters in DAVID COPPERFIELD. LIFE

Highgate Hill Bill Sikes went through Islington when endeavouring to escape after the murder of Nancy, and *strode up the hill at Highgate, on which stands the stone in honour of Whittington.* This may be seen on the left incorporated in a lamp post. OLIVER TWIST CH. XLVIII

Joe Willet, running from home and Dolly, *went out by Islington and so on to Highgate, and sat on many stones and gates but there were no voices in the bells to bid him turn.* BARNABY RUDGE CH. XXXI

Holborn *Chicken Smivey of Holborn, twenty-six-and-a-half B: lodger.* Address given by Mr. Tigg on behalf of Martin Chuzzlewit at the pawnbrokers where by chance they met and the latter, probably by help of the former, got his watch pawned. MARTIN CHUZZLEWIT CH. XIII

The lower (easterly) end of Gamages covers the site of the Black Bull in Holborn, where Mrs. Gamp and Betsey Prig nursed Mr. Lewsome *turn and turn about*, the latter by day, the former by night. MARTIN CHUZZLEWIT CH. XXV

Holborn Court See Gray's Inn, South Square.

Holborn Viaduct Completed 1869 across the hills which made this road so notorious in the coaching days. We can imagine Job Trotter *abating nothing of his speed* running up Holborn Hill to Mr. Perker's at Gray's Inn. PICKWICK PAPERS CH. XLVII

Also Wemmick, with *such a post office of a mouth* walking here with Pip, who had got to the top of Holborn Hill before he *knew it was merely a mechanical appearance, and that he was not smiling at all.* GREAT EXPECTATIONS CH. XXI

We can also see Oliver Twist trudging along here in company with Sikes en route for the *Chertsey Crib*, looking up at the clock of St. Andrew's Church, now half hidden by the Viaduct, and being told it was *hard upon seven! You must step out.* OLIVER TWIST CH. XXI

The distiller, Langdale, lived *on Holborn Hill* and *had great storehouses and drove a large trade.* He and Mr. Haredale went into the former's house by a back entrance to evade the rioters and later Joe Willet and Mr. Edward Chester also got in by the back to rescue Mr. Haredale and the distiller. BARNABY RUDGE CH. LXVI, LXVII, LXVIII

As much mud in the streets, as if the waters had but newly retired from the face of the earth, and it would not be wonderful to meet a Megalosaurus, forty feet long or so, waddling like an elephantine lizard up Holborn Hill. BLEAK HOUSE CH. I

Holloway Here the Wilfers lived; it must have been between the Holloway Road and the dust mounds at Battle Bridge (King's Cross), *a tract of suburban Sahara where tiles and bricks were burnt . . . rubbish was shot . . . dogs were fought, and dust was heaped by contractors.* Mrs. Wilfer, like Mrs. Dickens and Mrs. Micawber, had essayed fortune in a Ladies' School, and Mrs. Wilfer was no more successful, for the man who supplied the brass plate *took it off and took it away . . . as he had no expectation of ever being paid for it.* OUR MUTUAL FRIEND BOOK i, CH. IV

Horn Coffee House At No. 29 Knightrider Street is the Horn Tavern, on the site of the Horn Coffee House to which Mr. Pickwick sent a messenger from the Fleet Prison for a bottle or two (or *bottle or six*) of wine to celebrate Mr. Winkle's visit. PICKWICK PAPERS CH. XLIV

Hornsey In Hornsey churchyard, Betsey Trotwood's husband was laid to rest. DAVID COPPERFIELD CH. LIV

Hornsey is named as one of the places in which Samuel Pickwick, G.C.M.P.C., had made *unwearied researches.* PICKWICK PAPERS CH. I

Horse Guards Sam Tappertit on two wooden legs, shorn of his graceful limbs was by the locksmith's aid (Gabriel Varden) *established in a business as a shoeblack, and opened a shop under the archway near the Horse Guards.* BARNABY RUDGE CH. LXXXII

Tim Linkinwater *punctual as the counting house dial which he maintained to be the best timekeeper in London . . . (for Tim held the fabled goodness of that at the Horse Guards to be a pleasant fiction, invented by jealous West-enders), the old clerk performed the minutest actions of the day.* NICHOLAS NICKLEBY CH. XXXVII

Horsemonger Lane Opposite Borough Road is Union Road, where young John Chivery *assisted his mother in the conduct of a snug tobacco business round the corner of Horsemonger Lane.* The notorious gaol has given place to a recreation ground, the name of the lane has been altered to Union Road, and the little shop, the *rural establishment one storey high, which had the benefit of the air from the yards of Horsemonger Lane jail and the advantage of a retired walk under the wall of that pleasant establishment,* has been demolished. LITTLE DORRIT BOOK i, CH. XVIII, XXII

Dickens witnessed the last public hanging from the terrace opposite the prison, and wrote an impressive letter to 'The Times' on November 13th, 1849, protesting against such demoralising scenes in public. LIFE

Houndsditch Church In St. Botolph church at the corner of Houndsditch, Cruncher *received the added appellation of Jerry.* TALE OF TWO CITIES BOOK ii, CH. I

A single stride at Houndsditch church . . . and everything is entirely changed in grain and character. West of the stride, a table, or a chest of drawers on sale, shall be of mahogany and French-polished; east of the stride, it shall be of deal, smeared with a cheap counterfeit resembling lip-salve. UNCOMMERCIAL TRAVELLER: ON AN AMATEUR BEAT

Houses of Parliament It was in the old Parliament Buildings that Lord George Gordon presented his No Popery Petition in 1778. BARNABY RUDGE CH. XLIII

Dickens entered the House as a reporter in 1831, a post he relinquished in 1836. LIFE

There was unquestionably a Chuzzlewit in the Gunpowder Plot, if indeed the arch traitor, Fawkes himself, were not a scion of this remarkable stock. MARTIN CHUZZLEWIT CH. I

St. Botolph's Church, Aldgate

Household Words The office of HOUSE-HOLD WORDS, a magazine edited by Dickens, stood in Wellington Street opposite the Lyceum Theatre. The building was pulled down when Aldwych was constructed. LIFE

Huggin Lane While there is another Huggin Lane off Queen Victoria Street and either could have stood for the birth-place of PICKWICK PAPERS, that off Wood Street was generally accepted as the more likely for the far-famed opening of *The Club, so renowned in the annals of Huggin Lane.* PICKWICK PAPERS: ADVERTISEMENT

Hummums Hotel was at the corner of Russell Street, Covent Garden. This or the Piazza, also in Covent Garden, was probably the hotel where the *Finches of the Grove* used to meet. GREAT EXPECTA-TIONS CH. XXXIV

When Pip received Wemmick's warning, *Don't go home* at the Temple Gate, he *got a late hackney chariot and drove to the Hummums in Covent Garden,* in those times always open. GREAT EXPECTATIONS CH. XLV

See Covent Garden and Market.

Hungerford Market On the site now occupied by Charing Cross Station and Hotel stood Hungerford Market, a large two-storied building opened in 1833 for the sale of meat, fish, fruit and vegetables, and replacing an earlier market built in 1680. The hall had stalls for cheap prints, pictures, frames, walking sticks, shells and sweetmeats. Mr. Dick's lodgings in London were here over a chandler's shop. DAVID COPPERFIELD CH. XXXV

Hungerford Stairs Here was the Blacking Warehouse where Dickens worked as a boy. It was *the last house on the left-hand side of the way at old Hungerford Stairs* says Dickens in his autobiographical fragment. *It was a crazy, tumbledown old house abutting of course on the river, and literally overrun with rats . . . the counting house was on the first floor looking over the coal barges and the river. There was a recess in it, in which I was to sit and work. My work was to cover the pots of paste blacking first with a piece of oil paper, and then with a piece of blue paper, to tie them round with string, and then to clip the paper close to them making it neat all round until it looked as smart as a pot of ointment from an apothecary's shop.* LIFE

In going to Hungerford Stairs of a morning Dickens says, *I could not resist the stale pastry put out at half price on trays at the confectioners' doors in Tottenham Court Road, and I often spent on that the money I should have kept for my dinner, or bought a roll, or a slice of pudding.* LIFE

This experience, with some variations and different names, Dickens used in DAVID COPPERFIELD. Only much later in life did he give his biographer, John Forster, the true story of his own boyhood at the time of his father's imprisonment for debt. LIFE; DAVID COPPERFIELD CH. XI

Hyde Park and Hyde Park Place Dickens lived at 16 Hyde Park Gate, February to June 1862; 57 Gloucester Place, February to June 1864; 16 Somers Place, May to June 1865; 6 Southwick Place, March 1866, and 5 Hyde Park Place, January 1870, all in the Hyde Park area, and all now demolished. LIFE

It may have been the house in Hyde Park that Dickens had in view when Mr. Micawber mentioned a *terrace at the western end of Oxford Street, fronting Hyde Park, on which he had always had his eye, but which he did not expect to attain immediately as it would require a large establishment.* DAVID COPPERFIELD CH. XXVIII

When Magwitch announced himself to Pip as his benefactor he advised him *to look out at once for a 'fashionable crib' near Hyde Park in which he could have a 'shakedown'.* GREAT EXPECTATIONS CH. XLI

Rose Maylie stayed at *a family hotel in a quiet but handsome street near Hyde Park* when Nancy visited her and informed her of Oliver and Monks. OLIVER TWIST CH. XXXIX

. . . not more monotonous than The Ring in Hyde Park, and much merrier. . . . UN-COMMERCIAL TRAVELLER: IN THE FRENCH-FLEMISH COUNTRY

India House this building, to which Dickens often makes reference, stood in Leadenhall Street, at the corner of Lime Street, on the site now occupied by an insurance company. UNCOMMERCIAL TRAVELLER: WAPPING WORK-HOUSE

Insolvent Court The Insolvent Court and the Horse and Groom were both in Portugal Street; the latter was the scene of the meeting of the two Wellers with Mr. Solomon Pell. PICKWICK PAPERS CH. XLIII, LV

Islington A house in Terrett's Place, off Upper Street, is pointed out as the possible original of the lodgings of Tom Pinch and his sister, as it possesses the requisite *Triangular Parlour.* MARTIN CHUZZLEWIT CH. XXXVI

As the mail coach from Yorkshire *traversed with cheerful noise the yet silent streets of Islington, and giving brisk note of its approach with the lively winding of the guard's horn, clattered onward to its halting place hard by the Post Office,* John Browdie got his first astounded glimpse of St. Paul's – *there be Paul's Church. 'Ecod, he be a soizable 'un he be.* NICHOLAS NICKLEBY CH. XXXIX

Esther and Inspector Bucket, on their return from their search for Lady Dedlock, came *at between three and four o'clock in the morning into Islington . . . we stopped in a High Street where there was a coach stand.* BLEAK HOUSE CH. LIV

Oliver, after having run away from the Sowerbys, and having met and joined the Artful Dodger who gave him food and drink, passed through Islington on the last stage of his long tramp. Through Islington, too, at a later stage in the story, came Noah Claypole and Charlotte, already connected with Oliver, while Islington was to see Sikes the murderer in flight. OLIVER TWIST CH. VIII, XII, XLII, XLVIII

Jack Straw's Castle See Hampstead.

Jacob's Island The Dickens Estate, Parker's Row, Bermondsey, now occupies the site of Folly Ditch – Bill Sikes's home. This is where Sikes was hung in trying to escape. OLIVER TWIST CH. L

Johnson's Court At No. 166 Fleet Street, Johnson's Court, the offices of the old 'Monthly Magazine' were to be found. This magazine was the first to publish a contribution from Dickens's pen, the manuscript of which he dropped *stealthily one evening at twilight with fear and trembling, into a dark letter box in a dark office up a dark Court in Fleet Street.* LIFE

Johnson Street, Somers Town (now Cranleigh Street). At No. 29 Charles Dickens lived in 1825 whilst attending Wellington House Academy. It became a Children's Library eventually and was partly destroyed in the war. (Entirely rebuilt.) LIFE

Kensington The coach taking the Pick-wickians to Bath reached Kensington turnpike before Sam Weller spoke. PICKWICK PAPERS CH. XXXV

The man who died from eating crumpets in Sam Weller's story came from Kensington. PICKWICK PAPERS CH. XLIV

Soon after reaching Kensington, Bill Sikes and Oliver, on their way to Chertsey, were overtaken by a cart in which they secured a lift. OLIVER TWIST CH. XXI

Kentish Town Recalling the time of his and Dora's *ordeal of servants* David says that they had an *interval of Mrs. Kidgerbury – the oldest inhabitant of Kentish Town, I believe, who went out charing, but was too feeble to execute her conceptions of that art.* DAVID COPPERFIELD CH. XLIV

Illustrating the exceedingly poor lighting in London in the days of Barnaby Rudge (1775), Dickens says that robberies resulting in loss of life were a nightly occurrence and *few would venture to repair at a late hour to Kentish Town or Hampstead, or even to Kensington or Chelsea, unarmed and unattended.* BARNABY RUDGE CH. XVI

Kenwood See Hampstead.

Kew Bridge One of the places Dickens mentions in describing the route taken by Sikes and Oliver from the East End to Chertsey where a robbery was planned – *that crib at Chertsey*, as Fagin named the venture. OLIVER TWIST CH. XXI

King Street, Covent Garden. *There are real people and places that we have never outgrown, though they themselves may have passed*

away long since. . . . We miss a tea-tray shop, for many years at the corner of Bedford Street and King Street, Covent Garden, London, where there was a tea tray in the window representing . . . the departure from home for school, at breakfast time, of two boys – one boy used to it; the other not. MISCELLANEOUS PAPERS: WHERE WE STOPPED GROWING

Kingsgate Street The Central School of Art and Design at the corner of Southampton Row and Theobald's Road covers the site of Kingsgate Street, where Mrs. Gamp lived over Poll Sweedepipe's shaving establishment. *This lady lodged at a bird-fancier's, next door but one to the celebrated mutton-pie shop, and directly opposite to the original cat's-meat warehouse; the renown of which establishments was duly heralded on their respective fronts. It was a little house and this was the more convenient, for Mrs. Gamp being, in her highest walk of art, a monthly nurse, or, as her sign-board boldly had it, 'Midwife', and lodging in the first-floor front, was easily assailable at night by pebbles, walking-sticks and fragments of tobacco-pipe; all much more efficacious than the street-door knocker, which was so constructed as to wake the street with ease, and even spread alarms of fire in Holborn, without making the smallest impression on the premises to which it was addressed.* MARTIN CHUZZLEWIT CH. XIX

It was at Kingsgate Street that the famous tea party took place, with Mrs. Gamp the hostess and Mrs. Betsey Prig as her guest. After consuming a 'tuppenny salad' and a quantity of gin from a teapot, the two ladies have their final quarrel over Mrs. Gamp's fictitious friend, Mrs. Harris. MARTIN CHUZZLEWIT CH. XXXVIII

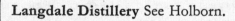

Langdale Distillery See Holborn.

Lant Street See Borough.

Leadenhall Market Bull's Head Passage, east of Gracechurch Street, takes one immediately to the west end of the market where the Green Dragon is supposed to have been the original of the Blue Boar, Leadenhall Market. Here Sam wrote the famous *Walentine*. PICKWICK PAPERS CH. XXXIII

It was to this Market that Captain Cuttle came, on taking charge of Sol Gills's premises in Leadenhall Street, to make arrangements with a private watchman there *to come and put up and take down the shutters of the Wooden Midshipman every night and morning*. The household duties of the little establishment were in the hands of *the daughter of the elderly lady who usually sat under the blue umbrella in Leadenhall Market*. DOMBEY AND SON CH. XXXIX, LVI

Tom Linkinwater boasted he could buy *new-laid eggs in Leadenhall Market any morning before breakfast* and accordingly *pooh-poohed* the idea of life in the country having any advantages over the city. NICHOLAS NICKLEBY CH. XL

Leadenhall Street Offices of Dombey and Son. See also India House. No. 157 (demolished) was said to be the original shop of Sol Gills, once occupied by Messrs. Norrie and Wilson, who moved to 123 Minories. The effigy of the *Little Wooden Midshipman* could have been seen carefully preserved inside the shop (now lodged, on loan, at the Dickens House, 48 Doughty Street, WC1).

Anywhere in the immediate vicinity (of the offices of Dombey and Son) *there might be seen ... little timber midshipmen in obsolete naval uniforms, eternally employed outside the shop doors of nautical instrument-makers in taking observations of the hackney coaches.* DOMBEY AND SON CH. IV

Leicester Place From the north of Leicester Square runs Leicester Place, where the Prince of Wales Hotel stood. Here Dickens gave a dinner in 1837 to celebrate the completion of PICKWICK PAPERS. LIFE

Leicester Square (Fields) Behind the National Portrait Gallery was Green Street (now Orange Street) where No. 10, since rebuilt, was said to be the original of THE OLD CURIOSITY SHOP.

Leicester Square was known as Leicester Fields in the days of BARNABY RUDGE. The rioters plotted to burn down Sir George Saville's house there. BARNABY RUDGE CH. LVI

It was *in that curious region lying about the Haymarket and Leicester Square, which is a centre of attraction to indifferent foreign hotels . . . racket-courts, fighting-men, swordsmen, footguards, old china, gaming houses, exhibitions, and a large medley of shabbiness and shrinking out of sight* that Mr. George in BLEAK HOUSE had his Shooting Gallery. BLEAK HOUSE CH. XXI

Limehouse To a visit to the lead mills *close to Limehouse Church*, Dickens devotes a chapter. UNCOMMERCIAL TRAVELLER: ON AN AMATEUR BEAT

Lizzie Hexam, with her father and young brother, lived in Limehouse. *The low building had the look of having once been a mill. There was a rotten wart of wood upon its forehead that seemed to indicate where the sails had been.* OUR MUTUAL FRIEND BOOK i, CH. III

Rogue Riderhood dwelt deep and dark in Limehouse Hole, among the riggers, and the mast, oar and block makers, and the boatbuilders, and the sail-lofts. . . . It was a wretched little shop, with a roof that any man standing in it could touch with his hand; little better than cellar or cave, down three steps. OUR MUTUAL FRIEND BOOK ii, CH. XII

See Six Jolly Fellowship Porters.

Limehouse Church Miss Abbey Potterson, proprietor of the Six Jolly Fellowship Porters *had been christened at Limehouse Church some sixty and odd years before.* Abbey was short for Abigail. OUR MUTUAL FRIEND BOOK i, CH. VI

Therefore I disembarked with my valise in my hand and waited for him (George Radfoot, his would-be assassin) *in the dark by that very Limehouse church which is now behind me.* OUR MUTUAL FRIEND BOOK ii, CH. XIII

The Captain himself was punctual in his attendance at a church in his own neighbourhood, which hoisted the Union Jack every Sunday morning; and where he was good enough . . . to keep an eye on the boys, over whom he exercised great power, in virtue of his mysterious hook. (This could have been Limehouse church which did, and still may, *hoist the Union Jack every Sunday morning.*) DOMBEY AND SON CH. XV

Lincoln's Inn Opposite Rolls Passage is Chichester Rents, at the far corner of which stood the old Ship Tavern, the original of Sol's Arms, *famous for its Harmonic Meetings – and its inquests.* Next door was Krook's Rag and Bottle Warehouse, *blinded by the wall of Lincoln's Inn.*

Mr. Tulkinghorn, going to Krook's, the rag and bottle merchant, calls on his lodger, a copywriter named Nemo, and finds him dead. Sol's Arms was the scene of inquests on both Nemo and Krook, the latter having met his end by *Spontaneous Combustion.* Krook used to get his daily gin – *Lord Chancellor's fourteenpenny* – at the Sol's Arms. BLEAK HOUSE CH. V, XI, XX, XXXII, XXXIII

Lincoln's Inn, the Undercroft

In Lincoln's Inn Hall, *At the very heart of the fog, sits the Lord High Chancellor in his High Court of Chancery.* BLEAK HOUSE CH. I

Here the memorable Jarndyce *v.* Jarndyce case dragged on to its long-delayed end. BLEAK HOUSE CH. LXV

'I am from Kenge and Carboy's, miss, of Lincoln's Inn' . . . *I asked him whether there was a great fire anywhere? For the streets were so full of dense, brown smoke that scarcely anything was to be seen. 'Oh, dear no, miss' he said. 'This is a London particular . . . a fog, miss', said the young gentleman. . . . We drove slowly through the dirtiest streets . . . until we passed into a sudden quietude under an old gateway and drove on through a silent square until we came to an odd nook in a corner, where there was an entrance up a steep, broad flight of stairs, like an entrance to a church. And there was really a churchyard, outside under some cloisters, for I saw the gravestones from the staircase window.* Kenge and Carboy's Offices were in Old Square. BLEAK HOUSE CH. III, XX

Serjeant Snubbin had his office in Old Square. PICKWICK PAPERS CH. XXXI

It is the long vacation in the region of Chancery Lane. . . . The Temple, Chancery Lane, Serjeant's Inn and Lincoln's Inn even unto the Fields, are like tidal harbours at low water; where stranded proceedings, offices at anchor, idle clerks lounging on lop-sided stools that will not recover their perpendicular until the current Term sets in, lie high and dry upon the ooze of the long vacation. . . . There is only one judge in town. Even he only comes twice a week to sit in Chambers. . . . No full-bottomed wig, no red petticoats, no fur. . . . Merely a close-shaved gentleman in white trousers and a white hat. BLEAK HOUSE CH. XIX

'Pray come and see my lodging' said Miss Flite. She lived close by . . . slipping us out at a little side gate . . . she stopped . . . in a narrow back street . . . immediately outside the wall of the Inn, and said, 'this is my lodging . . . pray walk up'. She had stopped at Krook's Rag and Bottle Warehouse where *she lived at the top of the house, in a pretty large room from which she had a glimpse of the roof of Lincoln's Inn Hall.* (Old Krook was Miss Flite's landlord.) BLEAK HOUSE CH. V

This is the garden of Lincoln's Inn said Miss Flite. I call it my garden. It is quite a bower in the summer-time. Where the birds sing melodiously. I pass the greater part of the long vacation here. In contemplation. BLEAK HOUSE CH. V

Lincoln's Inn Fields No. 58 was the original of Mr. Tulkinghorn's house, *a large house, formerly a house of state.*

G

It was also where Dickens's friend and biographer, John Forster, lived. Here Dickens read THE CHIMES to a select circle of friends, before its publication, coming from Italy specially for the purpose. BLEAK HOUSE CH. X; LIFE

David Copperfield's Aunt, Betsey Trotwood, being in

mortal dread of fire, took lodgings for a week *at a kind of private hotel in Lincoln's Inn Fields, where there was a stone staircase and a convenient door in the roof.* DAVID COPPERFIELD CH. XXIII

The Gordon rioters made use of Lincoln's Inn Fields in the course of their lawless gatherings. BARNABY RUDGE CH. L, LXIII

Little Britain Mr. Jaggers had written on his card that his address was Little Britain, *just out of Smithfield, and close by the coach office.* GREAT EX- PECTATIONS CH. XX

Little Wooden Midshipman See Leadenhall Street.

Lombard Street The office of Barbox Brothers was in a *dim den up in a corner of a court off Lombard Street.* CHRISTMAS STORIES: MUGBY JUNCTION

No. 58 Lincoln's Inn Fields

The Poor Relation used to take little Frank to walk in Lombard Street, on account of the *great riches there.* CHRISTMAS STORIES: THE POOR RELATION'S STORY

It was a rapturous dream of Mr. Dorrit, to find himself set aloft in this public car of triumph, making a magnificent progress

to that befitting destination, the golden street of the Lombards.
LITTLE DORRIT BOOK ii, CH. XVI

At No. 1 Lombard Street, was the banking house of Smith, Payne & Smith, later the Union of London and Smith's Bank. The elder Weller was handed *a cheque on Smith, Payne & Smith for five hundred and thirty pounds, that being the sum of money to which Mr. Weller at the market price of the day, was entitled, on consideration of the balance of the second Mrs. Weller's funded savings.* PICKWICK PAPERS CH. LV

The Manager of Smith, Payne & Smith was John Beadnell, who lived next door. His brother, George Beadnell, who later succeeded as Manager, was father to Maria who became Dickens's first love and from whom he parted after three years of stormy courtship. She was said to be the original of Dora in DAVID COPPERFIELD and later of Flora in LITTLE DORRIT. LIFE

London Bridge OUR MUTUAL FRIEND opens *between South-wark Bridge which is of iron, and London Bridge which is of stone, as an autumn evening was closing in.* The second London Bridge was designed by Sir John Rennie and built 1824–31. (Now transported to America and replaced by new bridge.) OUR MUTUAL FRIEND BOOK i, CH. I

Riah the kind Jew *passed over London Bridge, and returned to the Middlesex shore by that of Westminster,* recrossing it later the same evening with Jenny Wren. OUR MUTUAL FRIEND BOOK iii, CH. II

Mr. Haredale, when in hiding at his lodging in Vauxhall, usually came to London Bridge from Westminster by water, in order that he might avoid the busy streets. BARNABY RUDGE CH. XLIII

The elder Rudge crossed London Bridge for the City and Smithfield, after leaving the widow's house, which was *in a by-street in Southwark not far from London Bridge.* This would have been old London Bridge. BARNABY RUDGE CH. XVIII

Nadget disclosed that Jonas Chuzzlewit, after the murder, changed his clothes and came out of his house, *with a bundle ... and went down the steps of London Bridge and sank it in the river.*
MARTIN CHUZZLEWIT CH. LI

The steps where Nancy made her disclosures to Rose Maylie were those which *on the Surrey Bank, and on the same side of the Bridge as Saint Saviour's Church, form a landing-stairs from the river*. These stairs were a part of the bridge; they consisted of three flights (and were in consequence those of the new London Bridge opened in 1831). The chapter in which Nancy's visit to Rose Maylie, temporarily staying near Hyde Park, is recorded, also records the plan for further meetings, Nancy explaining: *Every Sunday night, from eleven until the clock strikes twelve . . . I will walk on London Bridge if I am alive.* OLIVER TWIST CH. XL, XLVI

After Bob Sawyer's supper party, Mr. Ben Allen accompanied Mr. Pickwick and the other three Pickwickians as far as London Bridge, on his way back *knocked double knocks at the door of the Borough Market Office, and took short naps on the steps alternately, until daybreak, under the firm impression he lived there, and had forgotten the key.* PICKWICK PAPERS CH. XXXII

David Copperfield made his first acquaintance with London Bridge in the company of Mr. Mell, who met him at the Inn in Whitechapel where the Yarmouth coach stopped, and conveyed him to Salem House on Blackheath, taking David on the way to see his own mother, in an almshouse over the Bridge, an incident that was to have serious consequences. DAVID COPPERFIELD CH. V

A year or two later, when Mr. Micawber was in the Marshalsea and David was working at the Bottle factory, he tells us that his favourite lounging place was old London Bridge. (This was the old one for Dickens was remembering his own youth in this story of DAVID COPPERFIELD.) *I was wont to sit in one of the stone recesses, watching the people going by, or to look over the balustrades at the sun shining in the water, and lighting up the golden flame on the top of the Monument.* DAVID COPPERFIELD CH. XI

David would meet the *orfling*, also up early and on her way to the Debtors' Prison, and tell her *some astonishing fictions respecting the wharves and the Tower; of which I say no more than that I hope I believed them myself.* DAVID COPPERFIELD CH. XI

Old London Bridge was a youthful haunt of Charles Dickens. LIFE

The Dorrit family – those able to leave the Marshalsea – constantly used the bridge; it was their most direct way to the City, though Southwark Bridge was equally so and for the west end too. But here a toll was charged which may have limited some in its use. LITTLE DORRIT BOOK i, CH. VII, XIV, XXXI; BOOK ii, CH. XVIII

The London Bridge mentioned in GREAT EXPECTATIONS CH. XLIV and LIV was the old London Bridge, which preceded the one opened in 1831.

London Coffee House No. 42 Ludgate Hill was once the London Coffee House, where Arthur Clennam sat on the Sunday after his arrival in London, watching people sheltering from the rain *in the public passage opposite, and listening to the bells ringing 'Come to Church, come to Church . . . they won't come, they won't come'.* LITTLE DORRIT BOOK i, CH. III

London Docks One may look in vain for *Number Thirty, Little Gosling Street, London Docks*, where Mr. F. breathed his last, as described by Flora Finching. LITTLE DORRIT BOOK i, CH. XXIV

This way came Mortimer Lightwood in search of news of John Harmon. *The wheels rolled on . . . by the Tower, and by the Docks; down by Ratcliff and by Rotherhithe.* OUR MUTUAL FRIEND BOOK i, CH. III

A particularly interesting description of the docks is to be found in UNCOMMERCIAL TRAVELLER: BOUND FOR THE GREAT SALT LAKE

London Hospital Sampson Brass informed Dick Swiveller that his sister Sally had found him a stool *in an open street just opposite the Hospital. She's a rare fellow at a bargain.* OLD CURIOSITY SHOP CH. XXXV

London Tavern This was at No. 5 Bishopsgate Street (now Bishopsgate). Here the first annual dinner of the General Theatrical Fund took place in 1846, with Dickens in the Chair. Five years later Dickens was again in the Chair here for the same Fund. LIFE

Here, too, we hear of the *Public Meeting of the United Metropolitan Improved Hot Muffin and Crumpet Baking and Punctual Delivery Company, capital five millions, in five hundred thousand shares of ten pounds each.* NICHOLAS NICKLEBY CH. II

London Wall Tom Pinch was lost here when wandering in the City. MARTIN CHUZZLEWIT CH. XXXVII

Clennam and Doyce shared part of a roomy house by London Wall. LITTLE DORRIT BOOK i, CH. XXVI

Long Acre Dick Swiveller was accustomed to getting his meals and articles of attire on credit. *This dinner today closes Long Acre* he said. OLD CURIOSITY SHOP CH. VIII

At No. 92 St. Martin's Hall, Dickens gave his first series of paid readings in 1858. The hall was burnt down in 1860, rebuilt and later reconstructed as the Queen's Theatre. It was converted into a warehouse about 1880 and the site is being redeveloped. LIFE

In considering what comes to the minds of people when brokers' shops are mentioned, Dickens says, *Their imagination will then naturally lead them to that street at the back of Long Acre, which is composed almost entirely of brokers' shops; where you walk through groves of deceitful, showy-looking furniture and where the prospect is occasionally enlivened by a bright red, blue and yellow hearth-rug, embellished with the pleasing device of a mail coach at full speed, or a strange animal, supposed to have been originally intended for a dog, with a mass of worsted-work in his mouth, which conjecture has likened to a basket of flowers.* SKETCHES BY BOZ: BROKERS' AND MARINE-STORE SHOPS

Long's Hotel The courier Baptista, a Genoese, tells the Story of the English Bride to his fellow couriers, beginning: *Ten years ago, I took my credentials to an English gentleman at Long's Hotel, in Bond Street, London, who was about to travel. . . . He engaged me by the six months.* REPRINTED PIECES: TO BE READ AT DUSK

See Bond Street.

Lothbury *The Pickwick Club, so renowned in the annals . . . is* connected with Lothbury and Cateaton Street. PICKWICK PAPERS: ADVERTISEMENT

Lyceum *His Majesty* (King of the Bill Stickers) hired a large hoarding opposite the Lyceum, *paid £30 for it, let out places on it, and called it, 'The External Paper-Hanging Station'. But it didn't answer . . . the Bill-sticking clause was got into the Police Act by a member of Parliament that employed me at his election. The Clause is pretty stiff respecting where bills go; but he didn't mind where his bills went. It was all right enough, so long as they was his bills!* REPRINTED PIECES: BILL STICKING

Lyons Inn An Inn of Chancery in Newcastle Street, demolished in 1863. The whole neighbourhood was swept

away in the Aldwych development. *Mr. Testator took a set of chambers in Lyons Inn where he had but very scanty furniture for his bedroom, and none for his sitting-room.* UNCOMMERCIAL TRAVELLER: CHAMBERS

Magpie and Stump See Clare Market.

Maiden Lane See Battle Bridge.

Manchester Buildings Westminster Underground Station occupies the site of Manchester Buildings, fully described in NICHOLAS NICKLEBY. Here lived Mr. Gregsbury, M.P., to whom Nicholas applied for a situation. NICHOLAS NICKLEBY CH. XVI

Mansion House *The Lord Mayor, in the stronghold of the mighty Mansion House, gave orders for his fifty cooks and butlers to keep Christmas as a Lord Mayor's household should.* A CHRISTMAS CAROL: STAVE ONE

There was a dinner preparing at the Mansion House, and when I peeped in at the grated kitchen window . . . my heart began to beat with hope that the Lord Mayor . . . would look out of an upper apartment and direct me to be taken in. MISCELLANEOUS PAPERS: GONE ASTRAY

Mr. Haredale rode up to the Mansion House to obtain the Lord Mayor's help in getting Rudge the murderer safely locked up till he could prefer a charge against him, only to

Mansion House

find another Catholic, Langdale the distiller, before him, imploring for help to protect his premises, threatened with fire for that night. To both, the Lord Mayor refused help, begging both to *go away* and not bother him, except at *proper hours.* The Commander-in-Chief, appointed to deal with the Gordon rioters, *endeavoured to arouse the magistrates to a sense of their duty, and in particular the Lord Mayor, who was the faintest-hearted and most timid of them all. With this object, large bodies of the soldiery were several times despatched to the Mansion House to await his orders.* BARNABY RUDGE CH. LXI, LXIII

Mark Lane *Rot and mildew and dead citizens formed the upper-most scent, while, infused into it in a dreamy way not at all displeasing, was the staple character of the neighbourhood. In the churches about Mark Lane, for example, there was a dry whiff of wheat; and I accidentally struck an airy sample of barley out of an aged hassock in one of them.* UNCOMMERCIAL TRAVELLER: CITY OF LONDON

Marshalsea Prison See Borough.

Marylebone Church A little beyond the site of Devonshire Terrace, on the same side of the road, is St. Marylebone Parish Church, accepted as the Church where the christening of little Paul Dombey and the second marriage of Mr. Dombey took place. Florence Dombey thought its bell so solemn at night.

There is a tradition that Mr. Tookey, the undertaker and parish clerk at the church, was known to Dickens.

Shop and firm still remain in Marylebone High Street. DOMBEY AND SON CH. V, XXXI

Maypole Inn See Chigwell.

Middle Temple and Gate See Temple.

Mile End and Gate *Mrs. Jellyby was in town, but not at home having gone to Mile End directly after breakfast, on some Borrioboolan business.* BLEAK HOUSE CH. XIV

During the riots, the party from Chigwell, on coming to Mile End, *passed a house the master of which, a Catholic gentleman of small means, having hired a wagon to remove his furniture by midnight, had it all brought down into the street to wait the vehicle's arrival and save time in packing.* BARNABY RUDGE CH. LXI

On the coach for Ipswich and passing the turnpike at Mile End, Sam dilates for Mr. Pickwick's entertainment on the strange life of pike keepers. PICKWICK PAPERS CH. XXII

One of the few people calling at the nautical instrument maker's shop was a woman who merely asked the way to Mile End Turnpike. DOMBEY AND SON CH. IV

Millbank Simon Tappertit married the widow of a rag and bone merchant of Mill Bank. BARNABY RUDGE CH. LXXXII

Mincing Lane Bella Wilfer calls on her father in his office in the firm of Chicksey, Veneering & Stobbles. Arriving in the drug flavoured region of Mincing Lane, she had the sensation *of having just opened a drawer in a chemist's shop.*

(The distinct smell of herbs could be clearly distinguished up to the last war. Bombing has caused the entire Lane to be rebuilt and that faint and fascinating odour no longer greets the wayfarer.) OUR MUTUAL FRIEND BOOK ii, CH. VIII; BOOK iii, CH. XVI

One church near Mincing Lane smelt like a druggist's drawer. UNCOMMERCIAL TRAVELLER: CITY OF LONDON CHURCHES; THE DICKENSIAN, SPRING 1948: CITY CHURCHES

The Mint Mark Tapley, in the States, irritated at ignorance shown as to just where the Queen lived, said she *usually lives in the Mint, to take care of the money!* Martin duly reprimanded him. MARTIN CHUZZLEWIT CH. XXI

Tom Pinch, on his way from Islington to the Monument, had decided that if he got lost he would call at the Mint or Bank of England, and, stepping in, *ask a civil question or two . . . confiding in the perfect respectability of the concern.* MARTIN CHUZZLEWIT CH. XXXVII

Monmouth Street Described by Boz as *the only true and real emporium of second-hand wearing apparel.* SKETCHES BY BOZ: MEDITATIONS ON MONMOUTH STREET

The Mint

Montague Place, WC1. Here Mr. Perker lived and here came Lowten with the news of the arrest of Mrs. Bardell for the costs which Mr. Pickwick would not pay. *Mr. Perker had had a dinner party that day, as was testified by the appearance of lights in the drawing-room windows, the sound of an improved grand piano, and an improvable cabinet voice issuing therefrom, and a rather*

overpowering smell of meat which pervaded the steps and entry.
PICKWICK PAPERS CH. XLVII

Montagu Square, WI. *Mr. Jorkins lived by himself in a house near Montagu Square, which was fearfully in want of painting.*
DAVID COPPERFIELD CH. XXXV

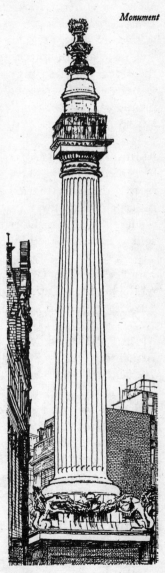

Monument

Monument *Surely there never was, in any other borough, city or hamlet, in the world, such a singular sort of place as Todgers's. And surely London, to judge from that part of it which hemmed Todgers's round and hustled it, and crushed it, and stuck its brick-and-mortar elbows into it, and kept the air from it, and stood perpetually between it and the light, was worthy of Todgers's. . . . The top of the house was worthy of notice. . . . For first and foremost, if the day were bright, you observed upon the housetops, stretching far away, a long dark path: the shadow of the Monument.* MARTIN CHUZZLEWIT CH. IX; THE DICKENSIAN, AUTUMN 1932: TODGERS'S

Behind the Monument the (church) *service had a flavour of damaged oranges, which, a little further down towards the river, tempered into herrings, and gradually toned into a cosmopolitan blast of fish.* UNCOM-MERCIAL TRAVELLER: CITY OF LONDON CHURCHES; THE DICKENSIAN, SPRING 1948: CITY CHURCHES; SUMMER 1948: CITY OF THE ABSENT

Tom Pinch was lost in wonder at the mysterious *Man*

in the Monument but lost faith in him, as a possible guide on his way, when he overheard his comments about the many steps to climb up after taking money for the ascent from a couple. MARTIN CHUZZLEWIT CH. XXXVII

Of the Monument Mr. F.'s Aunt sagely remarks, *it was put up arter the Great Fire of London and the Great Fire of London was not the fire in which your Uncle George's workshops was burned down.* LITTLE DORRIT BOOK i, CH. XIII

This was the place of *no temptation* recommended by the elder Willet to his son, when he gave him *sixpence . . . to spend in the diversions of London* – the diversions he recommended being *to go to the top of the Monument and sitting there.* BARNABY RUDGE CH. XIII

Monument Yard (A *paved yard near the Monument* not actually identified). Here Mark Tapley met his old neighbours from Eden in America and embraced them affectionately. MARTIN CHUZZLEWIT CH. VIII, IX, X, XXXVII, LIV

Here, too, Mr. Dorrit's solicitors, Peddle & Pool, are said to have had their office. LITTLE DORRIT BOOK i, CH. XXXVI

Moorfields The Gordon rioters went to Moorfields and, while burning Catholic-owned houses there, threw living canaries into the fires. BARNABY RUDGE CH. LII, LXVI

Mount Pleasant When Oliver was taken home to Mr. Brownlow's at Pentonville, *the coach rattled away down Mount Pleasant and up Exmouth Street.* OLIVER TWIST CH. XII

The Smallweed family resided *in a rather ill-favoured and ill-savoured neighbourhood, though one of its rising grounds bears the name of Mount Pleasant . . . in a little narrow street, always solitary, shady, and sad, closely bricked in on all sides like a tomb, but where there yet lingers the stump of an old forest tree, whose flavour is about as fresh and natural as the Smallweed smack of youth.* BLEAK HOUSE CH. XXI

Mutton Hill Later called Vine Street (now Vine Hill). Here was the Field Lane Ragged School in which Dickens took a great interest. LIFE

Young Oliver was brought down this Hill to the Hatton Garden Police Court, before Mr. Fang, magistrate. OLIVER TWIST CH. XI

New Cut Mr. Joe Whelks lived in the New Cut, Lambeth. MISCELLANEOUS PAPERS: AMUSEMENTS OF THE PEOPLE

New Kent Road After the *long-legged young man with the very little empty donkey cart standing near the Obelisk* had run off with David's box and his only ten shillings and sixpence, and David had given chase till he had no breath to call out, or continue the chase, he *faced about for Greenwich, which I had understood was on the Dover Road*, and commenced his weary journey down the Kent Road. DAVID COPPERFIELD CH. XII, XIII

New River Head (now Metropolitan Water Board Head Office – Rosebery Avenue). *The 'ouse that I am stopping at – a sort of private hotel and boarding 'ouse, Master Copperfield, near the New River 'ed – will have gone to bed these two hours.* DAVID COPPERFIELD CH. XXV

In the Gordon riots a special detachment of soldiers was detailed to guard this important area because of a threat to cut the main pipes, so that there might be no water for the extinction of the flames. BARNABY RUDGE CH. LXVII

Newgate Prison Dickens, in writing of Newgate, says that it was a new building, *recently completed at a vast expense, and considered to be of enormous strength*. BARNABY RUDGE CH. LXI

In a cell in Newgate, Lord George Gordon died on November 1st, 1793. BARNABY RUDGE CH. LXXXI

Newgate Prison was destroyed by fire in the Gordon Riots. BARNABY RUDGE CH. LXIV, LXV

Fagin was imprisoned and met his end here. OLIVER TWIST CH. LII

Kit Nubbles was wrongfully imprisoned here for a time. OLD CURIOSITY SHOP CH. LXIII

Dickens enlarges graphically on the tragedy that so many imprisoned there endure, only to end in violent death. Smike, for some reason, on his way back to Bow, *At the foot of Ludgate Hill, he turned a little out of the road to satisfy his curiosity by having a look at Newgate.* NICHOLAS NICKLEBY CH. IV, XXXVIII

Pip was taken by Wemmick into the prison, the latter having some business to see to there. Magwitch was to face his trial there, though already dying, but death mercifully released him from consequences of his undeserved fate. GREAT EXPECTATIONS CH. XX, XXXII, XXXIII

Boz gives us a detailed and most graphic account of a visit to Newgate, very well worth reading, for a glimpse of those days and for the pity and penetration the young Dickens displays. SKETCHES BY BOZ: A VISIT TO NEWGATE; CRIMINAL COURTS

Newgate Street Passing along the street, Sam remarked to Mr. Pickwick on the date fixed for the trial being February 14th. *Remarkable coincidence . . . Walentine's Day, sir, reg'lar good day for a breach o' promise trial.* PICKWICK PAPERS CH. XXXI

Newman Street, W1. No. 26 was the house of Mr. Turveydrop: *A sufficiently dingy house at the corner of an archway with busts in all the staircase windows. . . . We went upstairs into Mr. Turveydrop's great room which was built out into a mews at the back and was lighted by a skylight. It was a bare, resounding room smelling of stables.* BLEAK HOUSE CH. XIV

Norfolk Street, Fitzroy Square (now Cleveland Street). The Dickens family lived at No. 10 (now No. 22) about 1814–16. Dickens also lived here 1829–31. LIFE

Norwood Here Carker lived *in the green and wooded country near Norwood. It is not a mansion; it is of no pretensions as to size; it is . . . tastefully kept . . . within, it is a house of refinement and luxury. Rich colours, excellently blended . . . the furniture . . . devised to suit the shapes and sizes of the small rooms . . . and yet . . . there is something in the general air that is not well . . . as false as the face of the too truly painted portrait hanging yonder.* DOMBEY AND SON CH. XXXIII

Northumberland House As *a very small boy indeed, both in years and stature,* Dickens went to view the lion over the gateway of Northumberland House (demolished). MIS-CELLANEOUS PAPERS: GONE ASTRAY

Miss Malderton was as well known as the lion on top of Northumberland House, and had equal chance of 'going off'. SKETCHES BY BOZ: HORATIO SPARKINS

Obelisk Young Charles went to a house near the Obelisk, to have his clothes valued when his father was imprisoned in the Marshalsea and their home was sold up. There was a condition that a debtor had to disclose all wearable effects of himself and family before the official appraiser in the matter of his bankruptcy. LIFE

David had his trunk and his half guinea stolen here by the youth who had undertaken to carry the trunk to the Dover Coach for 6*d*. Unable to catch the *long-legged young man*, David commenced his journey on foot to Dover. DAVID COPPER-FIELD CH. XII

Those that are acquainted with London are aware of a locality on the Surrey side of the river Thames, called the Obelisk, or, more generally, the Obstacle. CHRISTMAS STORIES: SOMEBODY'S LUGGAGE

The Obelisk previously stood in the centre of St. George's Circus, formerly St. George's Fields, the scene of the massing of the Gordon rioters. BARNABY RUDGE CH. XLVIII

The attorneys to the Commissioners of the Insolvent Court had their residences usually on the outskirts of 'The Rules', *chiefly lying within a circle of one mile from the Obelisk in St. George's Fields.* Mr. Solomon Pell, one of this learned body, was a *fat, flabby, pale man, in a surtout which looked green one minute and brown the next.* PICKWICK PAPERS CH. XLIII

Obelisk, Lambeth Road

Old Bailey Bailey Junior was said to be one of the temporary names given to this promising youth by the *young gentleman* of Todgers's *in contradistinction perhaps to Old Bailey.* MARTIN CHUZZLEWIT CH. IX

Dickens writes in A TALE OF TWO CITIES, *the Old Bailey was famous as a kind of deadly inn-yard, from which pale travellers set out continually, in carts and coaches, on a violent passage into the other world.* Charles Darnay was tried here for treason and acquitted because of his likeness to Sydney Carton. A TALE OF TWO CITIES BOOK ii, CH. II

Old Curiosity Shop See Leicester Square and Clare Market.

Old Kent Road On the right as one enters the Old Kent Road a new building replaces the old Deaf and Dumb establishment to which Dr. Marigold took his Sophy for tuition. CHRISTMAS STORIES: DOCTOR MARIGOLD'S PRESCRIPTIONS

Somewhere in the Old Kent Road was Mr. Dolloby's shop where David sold the first portion of his wardrobe. DAVID COPPERFIELD CH. XIII

In this neighbourhood, too, no doubt, Bradley Headstone's School was situated, described as being *down in that district of the flat country tending to the Thames, where Kent and Surrey meet, and where the railways still bestride the market-gardens that will soon die under them.* OUR MUTUAL FRIEND BOOK ii, CH. I

Old Square See Lincoln's Inn.

Old Street In proposing to Esther Summerson, Mr. Guppy said – *My mother has a little property . . . in the Old Street Road. She is eminently calculated for a mother-in-law.* After his rejection he concludes – *In case you should think better – at any time, however distant, that's no consequence, for my feelings can never alter – of anything I have said, particularly what I might not do – Mr. William Guppy, eighty-seven, Penton Place, or if removed, or dead (of blighted hopes or anything of that sort), care of Mrs. Guppy, three hundred and two, Old Street Road, will be sufficient.* BLEAK HOUSE CH. IX

Opera Colonnade See Haymarket.

Osborne's Hotel See Adelphi Hotel.

Osnaburgh Terrace, near Regent's Park. Dickens lived at No. 9 for a time in 1844. LIFE

Oxford Market Close to Oxford Circus and near Great Portland Street was Oxford Market, where Towlinson, Dombey's butler, had *visions of leading an altered and blameless existence as a serious greengrocer.* DOMBEY AND SON CH. XVIII

Oxford Street It was in the neighbourhood of Oxford Street that Nicholas first saw Madeleine Bray at the General Agency Office, and here, later on, he first met Mr. Charles Cheeryble, who *dragged him back into Oxford Street, and, hailing an omnibus on its way to the City, pushed Nicholas in before him, and followed himself.* NICHOLAS NICKLEBY CH. XVI, XXXV

In the search for Miss Wade, Mr. Meagles and Arthur Clennam *rode to the top of Oxford Street, and there alighting, dived in among the great streets of melancholy stateliness . . . of which there is a labyrinth near Park Lane.* LITTLE DORRIT BOOK i, CH. XXVII

Mr. Boythorn leaving us within a week, we (Mr. Jarndyce, Esther, Ada and Richard) *to k up our abode at a cheerful lodging near O ‹ford Street, over an upholsterer's shop.* BLEAK HOUSE CH. XIII

Palace Yard Mr. Haredale, bent on his secret errand, and coming from his lodging at Vauxhall on his way to London Bridge via Westminster Hall and Palace Yard, unexpectedly came upon Sir John Chester and Gashford, secretary to Lord George Gordon. BARNABY RUDGE CH. XLIII

The Exchequer Coffee House, Old Palace Yard, was the address which Julius Handford (i.e. John Harmon) gave to the Inspector down by Limehouse. OUR MUTUAL FRIEND BOOK i, CH. III

Pall Mall Near Pall Mall *in a first floor over a tailor's,* were the main offices of *The Anglo-Bengalee Disinterested Loan and Life Assurance Company.* The Chairman of this company, Mr. Tigg Montague, who lived in Pall Mall close to his imposing offices, kept a cab, a spirited horse and Mr. Bailey Junior, the erstwhile Bailey of Todgers's. This versatile youth, out to exercise the horse, drove his master's cab as if it were his own *tempting boys, with friendly words, to get up behind, and immediately afterwards cutting them down . . . going round St. James's Square, at a hand gallop and coming slowly into Pall Mall by another entry, as if, in the interval, his pace had been a perfect crawl.* MARTIN CHUZZLEWIT CH. XXVII, XXVIII

In Pall Mall, Chops the dwarf, when *going into society,* had his lodgings and *blazed away* the lottery fortune. CHRISTMAS STORIES: GOING INTO SOCIETY

Twemlow gets to the Club by the appointed time. At the club he promptly secures a large window, writing materials, and all the newspapers and establishes himself, immoveable, to be respectfully contemplated by Pall Mall. OUR MUTUAL FRIEND BOOK ii, CH. III

Paper Buildings See Temple.

Park Lane Nicholas Nickleby attacks Sir Mulberry Hawk outside an hotel in a turning off Park Lane for making insulting remarks about his sister. NICHOLAS NICKLEBY CH. XXXII

Arthur Clennam and Mr. Meagles have an address near Park Lane in their search for Miss Wade and Tattycorum. LITTLE DORRIT BOOK i, CH. XXVII

Montague Tigg gives his address to the pawnbroker as 1542 Park Lane (a fictitious one). MARTIN CHUZZLEWIT CH. XIII

Parliament Street Dickens in the fragment of his auto-biography which he never completed said – *I remember one evening going into a public house in Parliament Street* (The Red Lion) *which is still there, though altered, at the corner of the short street leading to Cannon Row and ordering a glass of ale, the very best . . . with a good head on it. They asked me a good many questions as to what my name was, how old I was, where I lived, how I was employed, etc. To all of which, that I might commit nobody, I invented appropriate answers. They served me with the ale, though I suspect it was not the strongest on the premises; and the landlord's wife . . . bending down gave me a kiss.*

This story has its counterpart in DAVID COPPERFIELD when he asked for the glass of the *Genuine Stunning*. DAVID COPPERFIELD CH. XI

Peacock, Islington (demolished). This is the Inn from which the teller of the Holly Tree story started off on his Christmas coach ride to the North. It was a bitterly cold night, and, when he got to the Peacock, he tells us *I found everybody drinking hot purl, in self preservation*. CHRISTMAS STORIES: HOLLY TREE INN

The coach went off *amidst a loud flourish from the guard's horn, and the calm approval of all the judges of coaches and coach-horses at the Peacock*. NICHOLAS NICKLEBY CH. V

Peckham Walter Gay went to a weekly boarding school here. DOMBEY AND SON CH. IV

Mr. Feeder spoke of the dark mysteries of London and told Mr. Toots that he was going . . . to board with two old maiden ladies at Peckham. DOMBEY AND SON CH. XIV

Dick Swiveller was sent with a letter to Peckham Rye by Sampson Brass. OLD CURIOSITY SHOP CH. LVI

Referring to gales, the Uncommercial says *Peckham suffers more than a virtuous Peckham might be supposed to deserve*. UNCOMMERCIAL TRAVELLER: REFRESHMENTS FOR TRAVELLERS

Penton Place, SE17. At 87 Penton Place, Mr. Guppy lived. *'It is lowly', he explained to Esther, 'but airy, open at the back, and considered one of the 'ealthiest outlets'*. BLEAK HOUSE CH. IX

Pentonville This was quite a fashionable suburb when Dickens wrote of it. Mr. Brownlow lived in *a neat house in a quiet shady street near Pentonville*. OLIVER TWIST CH. XII

The private residence of Mr. Pancks was in Pentonville. LITTLE DORRIT BOOK i, CH. XXV

Mr. Micawber indited at least one of his many letters from his *residence, Pentonville, London*. DAVID COPPERFIELD CH. XVII

Mr. Nicodemus Dumps *rented a first floor furnished at Pentonville which he originally took because it commanded a dismal prospect of an adjacent churchyard.* SKETCHES BY BOZ: THE BLOOMSBURY CHRISTENING

The cabby, referring to the horse in which Mr. Pickwick is interested, says *he lives at Pentonwil when he's at home.* PICKWICK PAPERS CH. II

Petersham (Elm Cottage, now Elm Lodge). Dickens lived here during the summer of 1839. In a letter dated July 13th from here to Blanchard he referred to *these remote and distant parts, with the chain of mountains formed by Richmond Hill presenting an almost insurmountable barrier between me and the busy world.* THE LETTERS OF CHARLES DICKENS (Pilgrim Edition)

Dickens had previously stayed at Petersham for a time in 1836, whilst writing the VILLAGE COQUETTES, as shown by a letter to the composer, John Hullah, from Petersham, suggesting that Hullah should pay him a visit there. LIFE

Piccadilly Mr. and Mrs. Lammle were married at St. James's church, Piccadilly. OUR MUTUAL FRIEND BOOK i, CH. X

Riah, Fledgby's tool in the latter's moneylending concern, Pubsey & Co., goes one foggy day to the Albany, off Piccadilly, to see his employer. OUR MUTUAL FRIEND BOOK iii, CH. I

Mr. Micawber, in a moment of high expectation as a result of his advertising, decided that he would move if his hopes were fulfilled. *There would probably be an interval, he explained, in which he should content himself with the upper part of a house, over some respectable place of business – say in Piccadilly – which would be a cheerful situation for Mrs. Micawber; and where, by throwing out a bow window, or carrying up the roof another story, or making some little alteration of that sort, they might live, comfortably and reputably, for a few years.* DAVID COPPERFIELD CH. XXVIII

In the Gordon riots, the Lord President's House in Piccadilly was one of those where parties of soldiers were posted before daylight as the week wore on. BARNABY RUDGE CH. LXVII

Near the corner of Dover Street on the left was the White
Horse Cellar, an old coaching inn. It had been removed from
the opposite side of the way where it stood in Pickwick's
day. Here Mr. Pickwick and Sam Weller took the coach for
Bath, at which time Sam made the discovery that the coach
was owned by a Moses Pickwick, which was a fact, Moses
Pickwick being a well-known coach proprietor of Bath. Sam
asked his Master: *Ain't nobody going to be wopped for takin' this
here liberty, Sir?* PICKWICK PAPERS CH. XXXV

Esther Summerson was met by Guppy at the White Horse
Cellar. BLEAK HOUSE CH. III

St. James's Hall stood on the site of what is now the
Piccadilly Hotel. Charles Dickens gave his last reading here
in March 1870.

Chapman & Hall Ltd., Dickens's first publishers, were at
No. 193 Piccadilly.

Devonshire House was used for the production of 'Not
So Bad As We Seem', a comedy by Lytton in which Dickens
had a part and which was performed before Queen Victoria
on May 16th, 1851. LIFE

Polygon Harold Skimpole *lived in a place called the Polygon, in
Somers Town, where there were at that time a number of poor Spanish
refugees walking about in cloaks, smoking little paper cigars . . . it*
(his house) *was in a state of dilapidation quite equal to our expectation. Two or three of the area railings were gone; the water-butt was
broken; the knocker was loose; the bell handle had been pulled off a
long time, to judge from the rusty state of the wire; and dirty footprints
on the steps were the only signs of its being inhabited.* BLEAK HOUSE
CH. XLIII

The Dickens family lived at 17 The Polygon in 1829,
according to Forster. Other authorities say 1827–28. LIFE

Portman Square *The Podsnaps lived in a shady angle adjoin-
ing Portman Square. They were a kind of people certain to dwell in
the shade, wherever they dwelt.* OUR MUTUAL FRIEND BOOK i,
CH. XI

Poultry A description is given of the military firing on the Gordon rioters in this street. BARNABY RUDGE CH. LXVII

Putney Arthur Clennam on his way to visit Mr. Meagles at Twickenham, *went by Fulham and Putney, for the pleasure of strolling over the Heath. It was bright and shining there; and, when he found himself so far on his road to Twickenham, he found himself a long way on his road to a number of airier and less substantial destinations. They had risen before him fast in the healthful exercise and the pleasant road. It is not easy to walk along in the country without musing upon something!* LITTLE DORRIT BOOK i, CH. XVI

After the death of her father, Dora Spenlow went to live with her aunts at Putney. David Copperfield says – *How I found time to haunt Putney, I am sure I don't know; but I contrived, by some means or other, to prowl about the neighbourhood pretty often.* DAVID COPPERFIELD CH. XXXVIII, XLI

St. Mary's church, Putney, beside the river, claims to be the one Dickens must have had in mind for David's marriage to Dora. *The church is calm enough, I am sure; but it might be a steam-power loom in full action, for any sedative effect it has on me. I am too far gone for that. The rest is all a more or less incoherent dream. A dream of them coming in with Dora; of the pew-opener arranging us*

... of a few boatmen and some other people strolling in; of an ancient mariner behind me, strongly flavouring the church with rum; of the service beginning in a deep voice ... DAVID COPPERFIELD CH. XLIII (There is an excellent illustration of the interior of the church by Phiz in the book.)

Queen Charlotte Hospital (formerly in Marylebone Road). *'My dear Louisa'*, said Miss Tox, *'knowing your great anxiety, and wishing to relieve it, I posted off myself to the Queen Charlotte's Royal Married Females, which you had forgot, and put the question, Was there anybody there that they thought might suit?'* DOMBEY AND SON CH. II

Queen Square Richard Carstone had *a neat little furnished lodging in a quiet old house near Queen Square.* BLEAK HOUSE CH. XVIII

Quilp's Wharf Any of the many wharves opposite his house on Tower Hill might have been associated with Quilp. *On the Surrey side of the river . . . a small, rat-infested, dreary yard called Quilp's Wharf in which were a little wooden counting-house burrowing all awry in the dust as if it had fallen from the clouds and ploughed into the ground; a few fragments of rusty anchors. . . .* OLD CURIOSITY SHOP CH. IV

Ranelagh Gardens Between the Barracks and Chelsea Hospital, now incorporated in the hospital grounds, are Ranelagh Gardens. *Mr. Stryver inaugurated the Long Vacation with a formal proposal to take Miss Manette to Vauxhall Gardens; or failing that, to Ranelagh.* TALE OF TWO CITIES CH. XII

Ratcliff The Highway, at Shadwell, was in Dickens's day known as Ratcliff Highway. It is described as a *remote but genteel suburb of Ratcliff* from which Nancy had recently moved to Field Lane, where so far she was not known. She was, therefore, the obvious one to go in search of Oliver, who was locked in one of the cells attached to the magistrate's court. OLIVER TWIST CH. XIII

Look at a marine-store dealer's, in that reservoir of dirt, drunkenness, and drabs: thieves, oysters, baked potatoes, and pickled salmon – Ratcliff Highway. SKETCHES BY BOZ: BROKERS' AND MARINE-STORE SHOPS

The borders of Ratcliff and Stepney, eastward of London, and giving on the impure river, were the scene of this uncompromising dance of death, upon a drizzling November day. UNCOMMERCIAL TRAVELLER: A SMALL STAR IN THE EAST

Raymond Buildings, Gray's Inn. At No. 1, Dickens was employed as a clerk by a firm of solicitors in 1827, when, young as he was, he may have begun to collect data for his critical remarks on the law and lawyers! LIFE

Red Lion, Highgate. Dickens was lodging at *Mrs. Goodman's,* next door to the Red Lion, in 1832. The Red Lion, on the North Road, was demolished in 1900. LIFE

Red Lion, Parliament Street. See Parliament Street.

Regent's Canal Mr. Watkins Tottle was thought to have drowned himself in the Regent's Canal. SKETCHES BY BOZ: PASSAGE IN THE LIFE OF MR. WATKINS TOTTLE
Dickens wondered why people were always being blown into the Surrey Canal but not the Regent's Canal. UN-COMMERCIAL TRAVELLER: REFRESHMENTS FOR TRAVELLERS

Regent's Park Tony Weller referred to it as *Regency Park.* Dickens at one time lived at 3 Hanover Terrace and wrote part of GREAT EXPECTATIONS there. PICKWICK PAPERS CH. XLV

Regent Street *In a handsome suite of private apartments in Regent Street,* Lord Frederick Verisopht lived. NICHOLAS NICKLEBY CH. XXVI

Richmond *Mr. Tupman, when his friends married, and Mr. Pickwick settled, took lodgings at Richmond, where he has ever since resided. He walks constantly on the Terrace during the summer months, with a youthful and jaunty air which has rendered him the admiration of the numerous elderly ladies of single condition who reside in the vicinity.* PICKWICK PAPERS CH. LVII
'I'm going to Richmond', Estella told Pip. 'Our lesson is that there are two Richmonds, one in Surrey and one in Yorkshire, and that mine is the Surrey Richmond. The distance is ten miles . . . I am going to live at a great expense, with a lady there, who has the power — or says she has — of taking me about, and introducing me'. . . . We came to Richmond all too soon, and our destination there was a house by the Green; a staid old house where hoops and powder and patches . . . had had their court days many a time. Some ancient trees before the

house were still cut into fashions as formal and unnatural as the hoops and wigs and stiff skirts. One of the properties in Maids of Honour Row, Richmond Green, is thought to be the original of the house where Estella stayed. GREAT EXPECTATIONS CH. XXXIII

Maids of Honour Row, Richmond

At the top of Richmond Hill is the famous Terrace, at the Park end of which is the site of the Star and Garter, the renowned hotel where Dickens celebrated the completion of DAVID COPPERFIELD. Thackeray and Tennyson were in the party. (The site is now occupied by the Home for Disabled Soldiers, Sailors and Airmen.) LIFE

. . . anywheres about where he lost the tide – say Richmond (Rogue Riderhood). OUR MUTUAL FRIEND BOOK iv, CH. I

. . . we rode into town from Richmond. SKETCHES BY BOZ: MEDITATIONS IN MONMOUTH STREET

. . . the banks of the Thames are very beautiful at Richmond. SKETCHES BY BOZ: THE RIVER

Rolls Yard Behind Symond's Inn were Rolls Yard and Chapel, where Mr. Snagsby loved *to lounge about of a Sunday afternoon, and to remark (if in good spirits) that there were old times once.* BLEAK HOUSE CH. X

Roman Bath, Strand Lane. Here Dickens had many a cold plunge, as also did David Copperfield. DAVID COPPERFIELD CH. XXXV; LIFE

Rood Lane *From Rood Lane to Tower Street, and thereabouts, there was often a subtle flavour of wine: sometimes, of tea.* UN-COMMERCIAL TRAVELLER: CITY OF LONDON CHURCHES

Rowland Hill's Chapel At the corner of Union Street and Blackfriars Road hung the *golden dog licking a golden pot.* On the opposite corner was Rowland Hill's Chapel, sadly fallen from its former high position; in turns it had been a metal warehouse, cinema, and boxing ring. *There are a great many little low browed old shops in that street and some are unchanged now,* Dickens tells us. LIFE

Royal Exchange *We never went on 'Change, by any chance, without seeing some shabby-genteel men, and we have often wondered what earthly business they can have there.* SKETCHES BY BOZ: SHABBY GENTEEL PEOPLE

A similar experience was that of Pip, who said *I went upon 'Change and I saw fluey men sitting there . . . whom I took to be great merchants, though I couldn't understand why they should all be out of spirits.* GREAT EXPECTATIONS CH. XXII

Herbert, too, *when he felt his case unusually serious . . . would go on 'Change at a busy time, and walk in and out, in a kind of gloomy country dance figure, among the assembled magnates.* GREAT EXPECTATIONS CH. XXXIV

Quilp *made appointments on 'Change with men in glazed hats and round jackets pretty well every day.* OLD CURIOSITY SHOP CH. IV

There they were, in the heart of it (the City); *on 'Change amongst the merchants.* A CHRISTMAS CAROL, STAVE FOUR

Flintwinch *went about to other country houses . . . and on 'Change. . . .* LITTLE DORRIT BOOK i, CH. XXIX

Dickens, when a child, says *I found myself on 'Change, and saw the shabby people sitting under placards about ships. I settled that they were misers, who had embarked all their wealth*

*to go and buy gold-dust or something of that sort, and were waiting
for their respective captains to come and tell them that they were ready
to set sail.* MISCELLANEOUS PAPERS: GONE ASTRAY

Mr. Toots, not bearing to contemplate the bliss of Walter
Gay and Florence Dombey, explained to Captain Cuttle that
he might possibly be under the necessity of leaving the
company assembled at the Little Midship-
man to see *what o'clock it is by the Royal
Exchange.* DOMBEY AND SON CH. LVI

Rules See Borough.

Russell Square Across this Square,
Dickens used to walk from Somers Town
in the morning on the way to the Blacking
Warehouse *with some cold hotchpotch in a
small basin tied up in a handkerchief.* LIFE

Sackville Street, W1. Mr. and Mrs.
Lammle had a temporary residence here.
*It had done well enough, they informed their friends, for Mr. Lammle
when a bachelor, but it would not do now. So they were always looking
at palatial residences in the best situations and always very nearly
taking or buying one, but never quite concluding the bargain.* OUR
MUTUAL FRIEND BOOK ii, CH. IV

Saffron Hill, EC1. *In an obscure parlour of a low public-house, in
the filthiest part of Little Saffron Hill; a dark and gloomy den . . .
there sat, brooding over a little pewter measure and a small glass . . .
Mr. William Sikes.* This public house was *The Three Cripples,
or rather the Cripples: which was the sign by which the establishment
was familiarly known to its patrons.* Fagin and Nancy, Noah
Claypole and Charlotte also frequented this place. OLIVER
TWIST CH. XV, XXVI, XLII

Phil Squod tells Mr. George how he took on a travelling
tinker's beat in this district: *It wasn't much of a beat – round
Saffron Hill, Hatton Garden, Clerkenwell and Smiffeld and*

there – poor neighbourhood, where they uses up the kettles till they're past mending. BLEAK HOUSE CH. XXVI

St. Andrew's Church See Holborn Viaduct and Ely Place.

St. Bartholomew's Hospital Jack Hopkins was a student with Slasher the surgeon, and tells of the boy who swallowed the necklace who *makes such a devil of a noise when he walks about, that they're obliged to muffle him in a watchman's coat, for fear he should wake the patients.* PICKWICK PAPERS CH. XXXII

St. Bartholomew's Hospital

Betsey Prig, who nursed *turn and turn about* with Mrs. Gamp, was described as *of Bartlemy's: or as some said Barklemy's, or as some said Bardlemy's; for by all these endearing and familiar appellations, had the hospital of Saint Bartholomew become a household word.* MARTIN CHUZZLEWIT CH. XLIX

Mrs. Gamp, calling on Mr. Mould, the undertaker, for a recommendation to night nurse a case with her friend, Betsey Prig, *recommended from Bartholomew's,* obtains his promise to condone her taking the post. (She already day nurses old Mr. Chuffy, of the Chuzzlewit family, on Mr. Mould's recommendation.) Mr. Mould remarks after her departure: *She's the sort of woman now, one would almost feel disposed to bury for nothing, and do it neatly, too!* MARTIN CHUZZLEWIT CH. XXV

Arthur Clennam, on his way to St. Paul's, saw a crowd round a man who had been injured. Finding he was Italian, he tried to befriend him and accompanied him to St. Bartholomew's Hospital. The man was John Baptist Cavalletto. LITTLE DORRIT BOOK i, CH. XIII

St. Botolph's Church See Houndsditch Church.

St. Clement Dane's Church, Strand

St. Clement Danes Mrs. Lirriper was married in St. Clement Danes Church in the Strand. CHRISTMAS STORIES: MRS. LIRRIPER'S LODGINGS

St. Dunstan's Church Next to Clifford's Inn is the church of THE CHIMES. *High up in the steeple of an old church* (predecessor of the present one) *far above the light and murmur of the town, . . . dwelt the Chimes I tell of.* Outside the church was the beat of Toby Veck (or Trotty), the messenger, and here he used to trot up and down taking consolation from the bells. THE CHIMES

The old church with its clock and two giants – as seen by Maypole Hugh, David Copperfield and also by young Dickens in GONE ASTRAY – was pulled down in 1830 but rebuilt.

There is a reference to St. Dunstan's church in A TALE OF TWO CITIES BOOK ii, CH. XII

St. George's, Borough. See Borough.

St. George's Circus (Fields) See Obelisk.

St. George's Church, Bloomsbury. See Bloomsbury.

St. George's Church, Hanover Square. Mrs. Nickleby, in her imagination, married Kate to Sir Mulberry Hawk with great splendour at St. George's, Hanover Square. NICHOLAS NICKLEBY CH. XXI

St. Giles's See Seven Dials.

St. James's Church See Piccadilly.

St. James's Hall See Piccadilly.

St. James's Park Where Mark Tapley arranged an interview between young Martin Chuzzlewit and Mary Graham. MARTIN CHUZZLEWIT CH. XIV

The Park was also the scene of a long conversation between Clennam, Meagles and Daniel Doyce. LITTLE DORRIT BOOK i, CH. X

Dealing with the ultimate fate of Sally Brass, Dickens says it was *darkly whispered that she had enlisted as a private in the second*

St. Dunstan-in-the-West, Fleet Street

regiment of Foot Guards and had been seen in uniform, and on duty, to wit, leaning on her musket and looking out of a sentry-box in St. James's Park, one evening. OLD CURIOSITY SHOP CH. LXXIII

Here, too, Ralph Nickleby had an ominous meeting, standing under a tree because of rain, with Mr. Brooker, ragged and starving, who recalled some very derogatory incidents in their lives to support his plea for help in his present extreme poverty. NICHOLAS NICKLEBY CH. XLIV

St. James's Square *The abyss to which he* (Twemlow) *could find no bottom, . . . was the insoluble question whether he was*

Veneering's oldest friend, or newest friend. He had *devoted many anxious hours . . . in the cold gloom, favourable to meditation, of St. James's Square.* OUR MUTUAL FRIEND BOOK i, CH. II

St. James's Street Some Chambers at the corner here were the scene of one of the two Ghost Stories, told in the second chapter of CHRISTMAS STORIES: DR. MARIGOLD

St. John's Church, Westminster. Dean Stanley Street was formerly known as Church Street, Smith Square. Here the Doll's Dressmaker, Jenny Wren, lived with her drunken

St. John's Church, Westminster

father, her *bad boy, near a certain little street, called Church Street, and a certain little blind square, called Smith Square, in the centre of which last retreat is a very hideous church, with four towers at the four corners, generally resembling some petrified monster, frightful and gigantic, on its back with its legs in the air.* The building still remains, splendidly converted into a concert hall, but the *tree near by in a corner, and a blacksmith's forge, and a timber yard, and dealers in old iron* are things of the past. OUR MUTUAL FRIEND BOOK ii, CH. I

St. Luke's Church, Chelsea. Here Charles Dickens married Catherine Hogarth on April 2nd, 1836. He had celebrated his 24th birthday two months earlier. The first number of PICKWICK PAPERS had appeared one month before this marriage and from Chapter 10, when Sam Weller appeared, Charles Dickens never looked back. LIFE

St. Luke's Workhouse On the opposite side of the street to the Eagle Gardens, City Road (site now covered by a public house), stood St. Luke's workhouse. A little servant girl was employed at the Micawbers', in Windsor Terrace, at the time that the boy David lodged with this family, and she was, he says – *a dark complexioned young woman, with a habit of snorting, who was servant to the family, and informed me, before half an hour had expired, that she was a 'Orfling', and came from St. Luke's Workhouse, in the neighbourhood.* DAVID COPPERFIELD CH. XI

St. Magnus's Church On the night that Nancy had a secret meeting with Rose Maylie and Mr. Brownlow on London Bridge steps, Dickens describes the murky night while the girl, and the sinister figure following her, were still. *The tower of old Saint Saviour's Church, and the spire of Saint Magnus, so long the giant-warders of the ancient bridge, were visible in the gloom; but the forest of shipping below bridge, and the thickly scattered spires of churches above, were nearly all hidden from sight.* OLIVER TWIST CH. XLVI

St. Martin-in-the-Fields Church On the steps of the church, David Copperfield had that memorable meeting with Mr. Peggotty on the latter's return from his search for Little Em'ly. DAVID COPPERFIELD CH. XL

The district was known to young David Copperfield. In describing two pudding-shops he says – *One was in a court close to St. Martin's Church. . . . The pudding at that shop was made of currants, and was a rather special pudding, but was dear, two pennyworth not being larger than a pennyworth of more ordinary pudding.* This experience and others like it belonging to his own life in the Blacking Warehouse days, Dickens used in David Copperfield's story. DAVID COPPERFIELD CH. XI

See Hungerford Market and Stairs.

I came to the great steps of St. Martin's Church as the clock was striking Three. Suddenly, a thing that in a moment more I should have trodden upon without seeing, rose up at my feet, with a cry of loneliness and houselessness, struck out of it by the bell, the like of which I never heard. We then stood face to face looking at one another, frightened by one another. The creature was like a beetle-browed, hair-lipped youth of twenty, and it had a loose bundle of rags on, which it held together with one of its hands. It shivered from head to foot, and its teeth chattered, and as it stared at me – persecutor, devil, ghost, whatever it thought me – it made with its whining mouth as if it were snapping at me, like a worried dog. Intending to give this ugly object money, I put out my hand to stay it – for it recoiled as it whined and snapped – and laid my hand upon its shoulder. Instantly it twisted out of its garment, like the young man in the New Testament, and left me standing alone with its rags in my hands. UNCOMMERCIAL TRAVELLER: NIGHT WALKS

Close to the church stood the coffee shop visited by Charles Dickens as a boy. The inscription on the door, read backwards from the wrong side, MOOR-EEFFOC, always gave a shock through his blood. LIFE

St. Martin's Court (from Charing Cross Road to St. Martin's Lane). *Think of a sick man, in such a place as Saint Martin's Court, listening to the footsteps, and in the midst of pain and weariness, obliged despite himself (as though it were a task he must perform) to detect the child's step from the man's, the slipshod beggar from the booted exquisite, the lounging from the busy.* OLD CURIOSITY SHOP CH. I

St. Martin's Hall See Long Acre.

St. Martins le Grand From the coach stand here Mr. Pickwick took the *bob's vorth* to the Golden Cross at Charing Cross. PICKWICK PAPERS CH. II

St. Mary Axe, EC3. It would be quite impossible today to identify the *yellow, overhanging, plaster-fronted house* which was the office of Pubsey & Co., presided over by Riah, the Jew.

In the pretty roof garden on this house Lizzie and Jenny Wren loved to sit and talk. OUR MUTUAL FRIEND BOOK ii, CH. V

St. Mary-le-Bow Church See Bow Church.

St. Mary-le-Strand Church Dickens's father, John, married Elizabeth Barrow in 1809 at this church. He was a clerk in Somerset House hard by. LIFE

St. Olave's Church *It lies at the heart of the City and the Blackwall Railway shrieks at it daily. It is a small small churchyard, with a ferocious strong spiked iron gate, like a jail. This gate is ornamented with skulls and cross bones, larger than life, wrought in stone; but it likewise came into the mind of Saint Ghastly Grim that to stick iron spikes a-top of the stone skulls, as though they were impaled, would be a pleasant device . . . hence there is attraction of repulsion for me in Saint Ghastly Grim, and, having often contemplated it in the daylight and the dark, I once felt drawn to it in a thunderstorm at midnight.* The Uncommercial refers to it as one of his best loved churchyards. UNCOMMERCIAL TRAVELLER: CITY OF THE ABSENT

St. Olave's Church, Hart Street

St. Pancras Church (New) *The clock of New Saint Pancras Church struck twelve, and the Foundling, with laudable politeness, did the same ten minutes afterwards.* SKETCHES BY BOZ: THE BOARDING HOUSE

St. Pancras Church (Old) This is where Roger Cly, the Old Bailey spy, was supposed to have been buried. Here, too, Jerry Cruncher and his son came later *fishing* as Jerry called it – but with a spade; in other words, *body snatching.* A TALE OF TWO CITIES BOOK ii, CH. XIV

St. Paul's Cathedral and Churchyard. *There be Paul's Church.
'Ecod, he be a soizable 'un he be,* said John Browdie to his wife
on their honeymoon trip to London. NICHOLAS NICKLEBY
CH. XXXIX

As Ralph Nickleby *passed St. Paul's he stepped aside into a
doorway to set his watch and with his hand on the key and his eye on
the cathedral dial, was intent upon so doing, when a man suddenly
stopped before him. It was Newman Noggs.* NICHOLAS NICKLEBY
CH. III

*Master Graham and another were posted at Lud Gate, on the hill
before St. Paul's . . . all cavaliers of any quality or appearance were
taking their way to Saint Paul's churchyard.* MASTER HUMPHREY'S
CLOCK

*The great bell of St. Paul's was striking One in the cleared air,
when Mr. Lorry, escorted by Jerry, high-booted and bearing a lantern,
set forth on his return-passage to Clerkenwell.* A TALE OF TWO
CITIES BOOK ii, CH. VI

David Copperfield *varied the legal character* of settling
Clara Peggotty's affairs by *going to the top of St. Paul's*: not
that it afforded that good creature much pleasure, for, from
her long attachment to her work-box it became *a rival of the
picture on the lid, and was in some particulars vanquished, she
considered, by that work* of art. DAVID COPPERFIELD CH. XXXIII

David's aunt was accosted by her husband, much to the
surprise of David, to whom she said – *get me a coach, my dear,
and wait for me in St. Paul's Churchyard!* DAVID COPPERFIELD
CH. XXIII

Eugene Wrayburn, with Mortimer Lightwood, led the
schoolmaster, Bradley Headstone, to St. Paul's Churchyard.
OUR MUTUAL FRIEND BOOK iii, CH. X

Mr. Boffin, sitting in Mr. Lightwood's office, referred to
*the gentleman in the uncomfortable neckcloth under the little archway
in Saint Paul's Churchyard. 'Doctors' Commons',* observed
Lightwood . . . *'then you and Doctor Scommons, you go to work, and
you do the thing that's proper'* said Mr. Boffin. OUR MUTUAL
FRIEND BOOK i, CH. VIII

As Lord George Gordon rode from the Maypole Inn to
his home in Welbeck Street, they halted at St. Paul's Churchyard. Looking up to the lofty dome, Lord George shook his

head as if to say: *The Church in Danger!* which brought loud acclaims from the crowds. BARNABY RUDGE CH. XXXVII

In the course of the Gordon riots, Maypole Hugh, heading attack after attack as though he bore a charmed life, *rode at the head of a great crowd straight upon St. Paul's, attacked a guard of soldiers* and released prisoners in their charge. BARNABY RUDGE CH. LXVII

You're as safe here as if you was at the top of St. Paul's Cathedral, with the ladder cast off, said Captain Cuttle to Florence Dombey. DOMBEY AND SON CH. XLVIII

I read with my watch on the table, purposing to close my book at eleven o'clock. As I shut it, Saint Paul's, and all the many church-clocks in the City – some leading, some accompanying, some following – struck that hour. GREAT EXPECTATIONS CH. XXXIX

Arthur Clennam crossed by St. Paul's on his way to his mother's house. LITTLE DORRIT BOOK i, CH. III

Daniel Doyce suggests that Little Dorrit takes a ride with him towards St. Paul's Churchyard to obtain a marriage licence. LITTLE DORRIT BOOK ii, CH. XXXIV

St. Peter's Church, Cornhill. Here Bradley Headstone had his fateful interview with Lizzie Hexam. *The court brought them to a churchyard; a paved court, with a raised bank of earth about breast high, in the middle, enclosed by iron rails.* OUR MUTUAL FRIEND BOOK ii, CH. XV

St. Saviour's Church Nancy, afraid she might have been followed to London Bridge, suggested that Rose Maylie and Mr. Brownlow should go down the steps. *The steps to which the girl had pointed where those which, on the Surrey bank, and on the same side of the bridge as Saint Saviour's Church, form a landing stairs from the river.* OLIVER TWIST CH. XLVI

See London Bridge.

Indeed, saving that I know the church of old Gower's Tomb (he lies in effigy with his head upon his books) to be the church of Saint Saviour's, Southwark; . . . I doubt if I could pass a competitive examination in any of the names. UNCOMMERCIAL TRAVELLER: CITY OF LONDON CHURCHES; THE DICKENSIAN, SPRING 1948: THE CITY CHURCHES

St. Sepulchre's Church Between Snow Hill and Giltspur Street is St. Sepulchre's Church, the clock of which heralded the death of many a prisoner awaiting his end at Newgate opposite. During the Gordon riots we read *the concourse . . . waited with an impatience that increased with every chime of St. Sepulchre's clock, for twelve at noon.* BARNABY RUDGE CH. LXIV, LXXVII

Salem House See Blackheath.

Saracen's Head and Yard, Snow Hill. The Saracen's Head Inn, where Squeers had his headquarters, was three doors from St. Sepulchre's Church, and was demolished in 1868. A new Inn was erected at the foot of the hill and is now occupied by some offices. A bust of Dickens for a time adorned the doorway with plaques of scenes from NICHOLAS NICKLEBY. The original site is now a Police Station.

Near to the jail, and by consequence near to Smithfield also, and the Compter (temporary prison) *and the bustle and noise of the city; and just at that particular part of Snow Hill where omnibus horses going eastward seriously think of falling down on purpose, and where horses*

St. Sepulchre's Church, Newgate Street

in hackney cabriolets going westward not unfrequently fall by accident, is the coachyard of the Saracen's Head Inn. . . . When you walk up this yard, you will see the booking-office on your left, and the tower of Saint Sepulchre's church, darting abruptly up into the sky, on your right, and a gallery of bedrooms on both sides. Just before you, you will observe a long window with the words 'coffee-room' legibly painted above it. NICHOLAS NICKLEBY CH. IV, V

On arrival at the Bull and Mouth Inn, *hard by the Post Office*, John Browdie with his young wife and Fanny Squeers called a hackney coach and when all were in, told the coachman to '*gang to the Sarah's Head, mun*'. '*To the vere?*' *cried the coachman.* '*Lawks, Mr. Browdie!*' *interrupted Miss Squeers,* '*The idea! Saracen's Head!*' '*Sure-ly*', *said John,* '*I know'd it was something about Sarah's Son's Head. Dost thou know thot?*' '*Oh, ah! – I know that*', *replied the coachman.* NICHOLAS NICKLEBY CH. XXXIX, XLII

Savile Row *I have mentioned Savile Row. We all know the Doctor's servant . . . I saw him, one moonlight evening when the peace and purity of our Arcadian west were at their height, polk with the daughter of a cleaner of gloves, from the door-steps of his own residence, across Savile Row.* UNCOMMERCIAL TRAVELLER: ARCADIAN LONDON

Scotland Yard *is a small – a very small – tract of land, bounded on one side by the river Thames, on the other by the gardens of Northumberland House: abutting at one end on the bottom of Northumberland Street, at the other on the back of Whitehall Place . . . the original settlers were found to be a tailor, a publican, two eating-house keepers, and a fruit-pie maker; and it was also found to contain a race of strong and bulky men, who repaired to the wharfs in Scotland Yard regularly every morning, about five or six o'clock, to fill heavy waggons with coal, with which they proceeded to distant places up the country, and supplied the inhabitants with fuel. . . . But the choicest spot in all Scotland Yard was the old public-house in the corner. Here, in a dark, wainscoted room of ancient appearance cheered by the glow of a mighty fire . . . sat the lusty coal-heavers, quaffing large draughts of Barclay's best.* SKETCHES BY BOZ: SCOTLAND YARD

Selwood Terrace See Chelsea.

Serjeant's Inn, Chancery Lane. It has been wrongly stated in the past that the Serjeant's Inn to which Mr. Pickwick went prior to the Fleet Prison episode was in Fleet Street. In point of fact the Serjeant's Inn was that on the south-east

corner of Chancery Lane, where it joins Fleet Street, to
which those Serjeants formerly in Fleet Street proper, whose
Inn stood on the eastern side of the present Post Office,
were moved, when that Inn closed. This happened in the
mid-18th century according to Harben's 'Dictionary of
London'. The Hall was taken by the Amicable Association
Society in 1737. Moreover, in further confirmation, according to Chapter XL of PICKWICK PAPERS, Mr. Pickwick
remaining firm in his decision to go to the Fleet Prison rather
than pay Mrs. Bardell's costs, he was *carried off to Chancery
Lane. . . . There were two judges in attendance at Serjeant's Inn.*
In its turn, this second Serjeant's Inn was itself dissolved
in 1876, the Inn sold by auction in 1877 and eventually
pulled down. Modern buildings stand over the site, whereas
that of the original Serjeant's Inn retains some semblance of
having existed, although entirely rebuilt, being still apparently
used by lawyers, abutting as it does on to the north-eastern
area of the Temple. Having made his decision as mentioned
above, Pickwick was therefore conducted by hackney coach,
accompanied by Mr. Perkins, his lawyer, with Sam in
attendance, to Serjeant's Inn, for the purpose of obtaining
the necessary habeas corpus, or *have-his-carcase* as Sam would
have it. PICKWICK PAPERS CH. XL

   *The Temple, Chancery Lane, Serjeant's Inn, and Lincoln's Inn,
even unto the Fields, are like tidal harbours at low water. . . .* BLEAK
HOUSE CH. XIX

   On the way to the Fleet Prison, Sam, Tony and a bevy of
friendly coachmen stop for refreshments at Serjeant's Inn
coffee house, and thence in style to Sam's self-imposed
unconstitootional imprisonment. PICKWICK PAPERS CH. XLIII

Serpentine Mr. Augustus Cooper walks twice to the
Serpentine for the purpose of drowning himself and comes
back twice without doing it. SKETCHES BY BOZ: THE DANCING
ACADEMY

Seven Dials Even as a boy Dickens was much attached to
this area. Forster tells us he had a profound attraction
of repulsion to St. Giles's. *Good Heavens!* he would exclaim,

what wild visions of prodigies of wickedness, want and beggary, arose in my mind out of that place. LIFE

Where is there such another maze of streets, courts, lanes and alleys? SKETCHES BY BOZ: SEVEN DIALS

We . . . were soon immersed in the deepest obscurity of the adjacent 'Dials'. SKETCHES BY BOZ: MEDITATIONS IN MONMOUTH STREET

Nicholas and his sister Kate find themselves in *that labyrinth of streets which lies between Seven Dials and Soho,* and in the cellar of a house discover Mr. Mantalini, goaded by his nagging wife to turn the mangle. *I am perpetually turning like a dem'd old horse in a demnition-mill. My life is one dem'd horrid grind!* NICHOLAS NICKLEBY CH. LXIV

Seymour Street (now Eversholt Street). **Chapel** Dickens used to attend services in this chapel in the days before his marriage. LIFE

Shadwell The region of the opium den of EDWIN DROOD whither came John Jasper. *Eastward and still eastward through the stale streets he takes his way, until he reaches his destination: a miserable court, specially miserable among many such.* EDWIN DROOD CH. I, XXIII

Dickens paid a visit to an opium den in Shadwell, in company with his American friend, J. T. Fields, and wrote, a month before he died: *The opium smoking I have described, I saw (exactly as I have described it, penny ink bottle and all) down in Shadwell this last autumn. A couple of the inspectors of Lodging Houses knew the woman and took me to her as I was making a round with them to see for myself the working of Lord Shaftesbury's Bill.* LIFE

The den was probably situated in New Court, close to the church, on the site of which a playground now stands. J. T. Fields has put this visit on record: 'In a miserable court, at night, we found a haggard old woman blowing at a kind of pipe made of an old ink bottle; and the words that Dickens puts into the mouth of this wretched creature in EDWIN DROOD we heard her croon as we leaned over the tattered bed in which she was lying.' LIFE

Ship Hotel See Greenwich.

Shoe Lane The block of buildings on the left of Shoe Lane – proceeding southwards – marks the site of Field Lane and Fagin's House, swept away when Holborn Viaduct was built. OLIVER TWIST CH. VIII

If one man get out at Shoe Lane, and another at the corner of Farringdon Street, the little old gentleman grumbles, and suggests to the latter, that if he had got out at Shoe Lane too, he would have saved them the delay of another stoppage. SKETCHES BY BOZ: OMNIBUSES

Shooter's Hill See Blackheath.

Shoreditch Sikes and Oliver, en route for the burglary at Chertsey, *threaded the streets between Shoreditch and Smithfield,* Oliver having spent the night with Sikes somewhere in the former place, where Sikes lived. OLIVER TWIST CH. XXI

Six Jolly Fellowship Porters *The bar of the Six Jolly Fellowship Porters was a bar to soften the human breast. The available space in it was not much larger than a hackney-coach; but no one could have wished the bar bigger, that space was so girt in by corpulent little casks, and by cordial-bottles radiant with fictitious grapes in bunches, and by lemons in nets, and by biscuits in baskets, and by the polite beer-pulls that made low bows when customers were served with beer, and by the cheese in a snug corner, and by the landlady's own small table in a snugger corner near the fire, with the cloth everlastingly laid. . . . .* (Miss Abbey Potterson was sole proprietor.) *For the rest, both the tap and the parlour . . . gave upon the river.* OUR MUTUAL FRIEND BOOK i, CH. VI

The Grapes at Limehouse is one claimant to be the original of this public house. See Limehouse.

Smithfield Here Barnaby Rudge helped his father to get rid of his irons, riveted on him in Newgate where they had met unexpectedly. They had been released by the rioters. BARNABY RUDGE CH. LXVIII

It was Smithfield they were crossing (Oliver, Sikes and Nancy). OLIVER TWIST CH. XVI

. . . and so into Smithfield; from which place arose a tumult of discordant sounds that filled Oliver Twist with amazement. . . . OLIVER TWIST CH. XXI

Noah Claypole with Charlotte *crossed into Saint John's Road, and was soon deep in the obscurity of the intricate and dirty ways, which, lying between Gray's Inn Lane and Smithfield, render that part of the town one of the lowest and worst that improvement had left in the midst of London.* OLIVER TWIST CH. XLII

See also Little Britain.

Snow Hill The soldiers fired on the mob at Snow Hill in the Gordon Riots. BARNABY RUDGE CH. LXVII

The pavement of Snow Hill had been baking and frying all day in the heat. NICHOLAS NICKLEBY CH. XLII

Arthur Clennam went by way of Snow Hill to his lodgings. LITTLE DORRIT BOOK i, CH. XIII

Near to the spot on which Snow Hill and Holborn Hill meet, there opens, upon the right hand as you come out of the City, a narrow and dismal alley, leading to Saffron Hill. OLIVER TWIST CH. XXVI

See also Saracen's Head.

Soho and Soho Square Manette Street leads into Soho, via Greek Street. *The quiet lodgings of Doctor Manette were in a quiet street-corner not far from Soho Square.* No. 10 Carlisle Street was generally supposed to be that house. *A quainter corner than the corner where the Doctor lived was not to be found in London. There was no way through it, and the front windows of the Doctor's lodgings commanded a pleasant little vista of street that had a congenial air of retirement on it. . . . It was a cool spot, staid but cheerful, a wonderful place for echoes, and a very harbour from the raging streets. . . . In a building at the back. . . church-organs claimed to be made, and silver to be chased, and likewise gold to be beaten by some mysterious giant who had a golden arm starting out of the wall of the front hall – as if he had beaten himself previous, and menaced a similar conversion of all visitors.* (This golden arm, a goldbeater's sign, is now in the Dickens House Museum, 48 Doughty Street.)

No. 1 Greek Street, the House of St. Barnabas-in-Soho, has since made quite a convincing claim to be the original of Dr. Manette's house. A TALE OF TWO CITIES BOOK ii, CH. VI

On the north side of the Square, a curious colony of mountaineers has long been enclosed within that small flat London

district of Soho. Here Obenreizer lived in a house that was a bit of *domestic Switzerland* shielding the beautiful Miss Marguerite and the mysterious Madame Dor, her elderly companion. CHRISTMAS STORIES: NO THOROUGHFARE

Soho Square is referred to as *a quiet place in the neighbourhood of Newman Street,* where Caddy Jellyby met Esther and walked round the garden in the centre of the Square. BLEAK HOUSE CH. XXIII

Near Carlisle Street stood Carlisle House where Emma Haredale met her uncle attending one of the Masquerades. BARNABY RUDGE CH. IV

Sol's Arms See Lincoln's Inn.

Somerset House Charles Dickens's father, John, when about nineteen years old, was appointed by Canning to a post in Somerset House, probably through Lord Crewe's influence. John's father had been steward at Crewe Hall. John Dickens had a clerical post in the Navy Pay Office at £80 per annum, later raised to £100 per annum. At the time of his imprisonment for debt his salary had mounted to £350 per annum. LIFE

Somers Town Snawley took lodgings in Somers Town and Squeers stayed with him. NICHOLAS NICKLEBY CH. XXXVIII

Southampton Street (now Southampton Place). Here came Mr. Grewgious to look for a lodging for Rosa Bud. *At length he bethought himself of a widowed cousin, divers times removed, of Mr. Bazzard's, who had once solicited his influence in the lodger world, and who lived in Southampton Street, Bloomsbury Square. This lady's name, stated in uncompromising capitals of considerable size on a brass doorplate and yet not lucidly as to sex or condition, was Billickin.... It is not Bond Street nor yet St. James's Palace; but it is not pretended that it is. Neither is it attempted to be denied – for why should it? – that the Arching leads to a mews. Mewses must exist.* EDWIN DROOD CH. XXII

Southwark Having rescued young Mr. Edward Chester whom he had found wounded and unconscious, and whom he had carried, accompanied by Barnaby, to the house of the latter's mother, not far off, Mr. Gabriel Varden the following evening set off to see how the young gentleman fared. *The house where he had left him was in a by-street in Southwark, not far from London Bridge,* and he was soon knocking at Mrs. Rudge's door. BARNABY RUDGE CH. V

See Borough.

Southwark Bridge OUR MUTUAL FRIEND opens *between Southwark Bridge which is of iron, and London Bridge which is of stone.* . . . This bridge at Southwark carried a penny toll until 1864, was designed by Sir John Rennie and built 1815–19. OUR MUTUAL FRIEND BOOK i, CH. I

One day young Charles Dickens was taken ill at the Blacking factory and it was decided he must go home. His father was at that time in the Marshalsea Prison and Dickens recorded the following incident in the scrap of his unfinished autobiography – *Bob (who was much bigger and older than I) did not like the idea of my going home alone, and took me under his protection. I was too proud to let him know about the prison; and after making several efforts to get rid of him, to all of which Bob Fagin in his goodness was deaf, shook hands with him on the steps of a house near Southwark Bridge, on the Surrey side, making believe that I lived there. As a finishing piece of reality, in case of him looking back, I knocked at the door, I recollect, and asked when the woman opened it if that was Mr. Robert Fagin's house?* LIFE (Dickens used Bob Fagin's name in the creation of Fagin in OLIVER TWIST.)

John Chivery proposed to Little Dorrit on Southwark Bridge and she also met Arthur Clennam on the bridge. LITTLE DORRIT BOOK i, CH. IX, XVIII

Spaniards Inn, Hampstead. Mrs. and Master Bardell and Mrs. Raddle, together with Mr. Raddle and friends, spent an afternoon at the Spaniards Inn where the former lady was traced by Mr. Jackson, clerk to Dodson & Fogg. He conveyed Mrs. Bardell to the Fleet Prison for the costs in the

Bardell *v*. Pickwick trial, which she had committed herself to pay. PICKWICK PAPERS CH. XLVI

Spaniards Inn, Hampstead

Spitalfields Fagin went via Spitalfields to Bill Sikes's place at Bethnal Green. OLIVER TWIST CH. XIX

In a dirty court in Spitalfields, the Uncommercial Traveller found the goldfinch who drew his own water in a little bucket. UNCOMMERCIAL TRAVELLER: SHY NEIGHBOURHOODS

Stagg's Gardens The building of the L. & N.W. Railway, Euston Station, and the goods yard at Camden, prompted Dickens to go into detail when he introduced us to the Toodles family at Stagg's Gardens: *This euphonious locality was situated in a suburb, known by the inhabitants of Stagg's Gardens by the name of Camberling Town . . . Camden Town. . . . The first shock of a great earthquake had just at that period, rent the whole neighbourhood to its centre. . . . Houses were knocked down; streets broken through and stopped. . . . In short, the yet unfinished and unopened railroad was in progress. . . . But as yet, the neighbourhood was shy to own the railroad.* DOMBEY AND SON CH. VI

But later, when Walter Gay went to find Polly Toodles, to bring some consolation to the dying Paul, he found a great change had taken place. *There was no such place as Stagg's*

Gardens. It had vanished from the earth. DOMBEY AND SON CH. XV

A few years after the publication of DOMBEY AND SON, Dickens wrote an article entitled AN UNSETTLED NEIGHBOUR-HOOD, showing how *It has ever since been unable to settle down to any one thing, and will never settle down again. The Railroad has done it all.* MISCELLANEOUS PAPERS: AN UNSETTLED NEIGHBOURHOOD

Stamford Hill Mr. Minns's only relation in or near London, Mr. Octavius Budden, *had purchased a cottage in the vicinity of Stamford Hill.* SKETCHES BY BOZ: MR. MINNS AND HIS COUSIN

Standard Theatre Nearly opposite Shoreditch church is what was formerly the Standard Theatre or The People's Theatre, to which reference is made in MISCELLANEOUS PAPERS: THE AMUSEMENTS OF THE PEOPLE

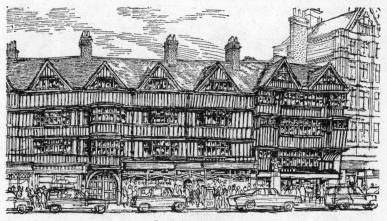

Staple Inn, Holborn

Staple Inn Opposite the southern end of Gray's Inn Road a little group of picturesque houses is to be seen, behind which lies Staple Inn, particularly recalling EDWIN DROOD. *Behind the most ancient part of Holborn, London, where certain gabled houses some centuries of age still stand looking on the public way, as if disconsolately looking for the Old Bourne that has long run dry, is a little nook composed of two irregular quadrangles, called Staple Inn. It is one of those nooks, the turning into which out of the* *clashing street, imparts to the relieved pedestrian the sensation of having put cotton in his ears, and velvet soles on his boots. It is one of those nooks where a few smoky sparrows twitter in smoky trees, as though they called to one another, 'Let us play at country', and where a few feet of garden-mould and a few yards of gravel enable them to do that refreshing violence to their tiny understandings. . . . Moreover, it is one of those little nooks which are legal nooks; and it contains a little Hall, with a little lantern in its roof.* EDWIN DROOD CH. XI, XVII, XX, XXII

Mr. Snagsby being in his way rather a meditative and poetical man loved *to walk in Staple Inn in the summertime and to observe how countrified the sparrows and the leaves are.* BLEAK HOUSE CH. X

Behind the first courtyard, restored after severe war damage, is a second, containing the hall of the Inn, and a house that presented *in black and white over its ugly portal the mysterious inscription:*

P

J   T

1747

In which set of chambers, never having troubled his head about the inscription, unless to bethink himself at odd times on glancing up at it, that haply it might mean Perhaps John Thomas, or Perhaps Joe Tyler, sat Mr. Grewgious writing by his fire. (This Court and the hall has been wonderfully restored, including the inscription over the doorway.) EDWIN DROOD CH. XI

Here, too, was the scene of the 'Magic Beanstalk Country' at Mr. Tartar's Chambers. *The top set in the house, the neatest, the cleanest and the best-ordered chambers ever seen under the sun, moon and stars. . . . No man-of-war was ever kept more spick and span from careless touch. . . . A neat awning was rigged over Mr. Tartar's flower garden, as only a sailor could rig it.* EDWIN DROOD CH. XXI, XXII

Star and Garter See Richmond.

Stepney To which Silas Wegg referred when he asked, *Would Stepney Fields be considered intrusive? If not remote enough, I can go remoter.* OUR MUTUAL FRIEND BOOK i, CH. XV

Stock Exchange Where *a sporting taste (originating generally in bets of new hats) is much in vogue.* DOMBEY AND SON CH. XIII

The two Wellers proceeded from the Bank to the gate of the Stock Exchange, to which Wilkins Flasher, Esquire, after a short absence, returned with a cheque on Smith, Payne & Smith, for five hundred and thirty pounds; that being the sum of money to which Mr. Weller at the market price of the day, was entitled, in consideration of the balance of the second Mrs. Weller's funded savings. PICKWICK PAPERS CH. LV

Or is it, asked the gentleman in the small clothes next door, at Bow, *in consequence of the statue at Charing Cross having been lately seen on the Stock Exchange at midnight, walking arm-in-arm with the Pump from Aldgate, in a riding habit?* NICHOLAS NICKLEBY CH. XLI

Stoke Newington The Uncommercial Traveller makes the fictitious supposition that evidence might be found in Shakespeare's works to prove that his uncle by his mother's side lived for some years at Stoke Newington. UNCOMMERCIAL TRAVELLER: DULLBOROUGH TOWN

Strand The offices of the 'Morning Chronicle' where Dickens was a reporter were at No. 332 Strand (now demolished). LIFE

We walked down the Strand, a Sunday or two ago, behind a little group; and they furnished food for our amusement the whole way. They had come out of some part of the city; it was between three and four o'clock in the afternoon; and they were on their way to the Park. SKETCHES BY BOZ: THOUGHTS ABOUT PEOPLE

On the day of David Copperfield's party at Mrs. Crupp's, going along the Strand and *observing a hard mottled substance in the window of a ham and beef shop, which resembled marble, but was labelled Mock Turtle, I went in and bought a slab of it.* DAVID COPPERFIELD CH. XXIV

Ralph Nickleby *made the best of his way to the Strand* to visit Miss La Creevy, and *stopped at a private door about halfway down the crowded thoroughfare. A miniature painter lived there, for there was a large gilt frame upon the street door.* NICHOLAS NICKLEBY CH. III

Mr. Haredale *walked along the Strand* after the burning of the Warren by the rioters. BARNABY RUDGE CH. LXVI

Bradley Headstone, with Rogue Riderhood at his side, also *walked along the Strand* on an eventful occasion, the former meditating, the latter muttering. OUR MUTUAL FRIEND BOOK iii, CH. XI

Arthur Clennam, *passing at nightfall along the Strand, and the lamplighter going on before him* saw Tattycoram and Rigaud. LITTLE DORRIT BOOK ii, CH. IX

Young Martin Chuzzlewit, having arrived an hour before dawn at the Adelphi, secured a room in an obscure public house, had a sleep and awoke to find it growing dusk again. He decided that he must pawn his watch and started out for this purpose. *He passed more Golden Balls than all the jugglers in Europe have juggled with in the course of their united performances, before he could determine in favour of any particular shop where those symbols were displayed.* (He was evidently walking along the Strand.) MARTIN CHUZZLEWIT CH. XIII

Having returned from the States with Mark Tapley, Martin Chuzzlewit set out to look for lodgings for both of them which he found *in a court in the Strand, not far from Temple Bar.* MARTIN CHUZZLEWIT CH. XLVIII

After the crowd at Temple Bar had mobbed the hearse of the spy, *The remodelled procession started, with a chimney-sweep driving the hearse . . . and with a pieman . . . driving the mourning coach. A bear-leader . . . was impressed as an additional ornament, before the cavalcade had gone far down the Strand.* A TALE OF TWO CITIES BOOK ii, CH. XIV

Dick Swiveller in referring to the necessity of him living on credit said – *There's only one avenue to the Strand left open now, I shall have to stop up at that tonight with a pair of gloves. . . . In about a month's time, unless my aunt sends me a remittance, I shall have to go three or four miles out of town to get over the way.* OLD CURIOSITY SHOP CH. VIII

Sun Court Dickens made a curious error when he said that Dodson & Fogg's clerk *bent his steps direct to Sun Court, and walking straight into the George and Vulture, demanded to know whether one Mr. Pickwick was within.* Sun Court was at 68

Cornhill, whereas the George and Vulture would be approached on the opposite side of the way, by St. Michael's Alley, at 42 Cornhill, or could be found by going up George Yard, Lombard Street. PICKWICK PAPERS CH. XXXI

Sun Street, EC2. Sikes and Oliver turned down Sun Street on their way to the robbery at Chertsey. OLIVER TWIST CH. XXI

Surrey Street, Strand. Mentioned by Mrs. Lirriper as inferior to Norfolk Street, in which her lodgings were situated. CHRISTMAS STORIES: MRS. LIRRIPER'S LODGINGS

Surrey Theatre (now demolished). Where *Frederick Dorrit played . . . a clarinet as dirty as himself,* and Fanny Dorrit danced. LITTLE DORRIT BOOK i, CH. VII

Here, too, on November 19th, 1838, an unauthorised version of OLIVER TWIST was staged. Dickens attended it and was so annoyed that 'in the middle of the first scene he laid himself down upon the floor in a corner of the box and never rose from it until the drop scene fell'. LIFE

Swallow Street Lord George Gordon rode up Swallow Street into the Oxford Road having come to London from Chigwell. BARNABY RUDGE CH. XXXVII

Symond's Inn This inn occupied the site of Lonsdale Chambers and the side of it backed on to Breams Buildings. Dickens's situation as an office boy was with Molloy, a solicitor who had his offices here in 1827. LIFE

In BLEAK HOUSE what in all probability were the same offices were assigned to Mr. Vholes. It was *a little, pale, wall-eyed, woe-begone inn, like a large dustbin of two compartments and a sifter. It looks as if Symond were a sparing man in his way, and constructed his inn of old building materials which took kindly to the dry rot and to dirt and all things decaying and dismal, and perpetuated Symond's memory with congenial shabbiness. Quartered in this dingy hatchment commemorative of Symond, are the legal bearings of Mr. Vholes.* BLEAK HOUSE CH. XXXIX

Next door to Vholes's office, Richard Carstone had taken apartments and here Esther came to see him, accompanied by Ada, and here she learnt that Richard and Ada had been married for two months. BLEAK HOUSE CH. LI

Tavistock House, Tavistock Square. Dickens lived here in 1851–1860. The offices of the British Medical Association now occupy the site, which is marked by a plaque. LIFE

Tavistock Street Mr. Minns *occupied a first floor in Tavistock Street, Covent Garden, where he had resided for twenty years, having been in the habit of quarrelling with his landlord the whole time: regularly giving notice of his intention to quit on the first day of every quarter, and as regularly countermanding it on the second.* SKETCHES BY BOZ: MR. MINNS AND HIS COUSIN

Tellson's Bank, Fleet Street. No. 1 Fleet Street marks the site of the older premises which Dickens calls Tellson's Bank in A TALE OF TWO CITIES. Actually Child's Bank at the time, it was demolished in 1879, but now rebuilt.

Tellson's Bank by Temple Bar was an old fashioned place.... It was very small, very dark, very ugly, very incommodious ... the triumphant perfection of inconvenience. After bursting open a door of idiotic obstinacy with a weak rattle in its throat, you fell into Tellson's down two steps, and came to your senses in a miserable little shop with two little counters, where the oldest of men made your cheque shake as if the wind rustled it, while they examined the signature by the dingiest of windows. A TALE OF TWO CITIES BOOK ii, CH. I

In *the musty back closet where Mr. Lorry sat at great books ruled for figures, with perpendicular iron bars at his window as if that were ruled for figures too, and everything under the clouds were a sum.* A TALE OF TWO CITIES BOOK ii, CH. XII

Outside the Bank, Jerry Cruncher, odd job man, sat on a *wooden stool made out of a broken-backed chair cut down,* a character *as well known to Fleet Street and the Temple as the Bar itself – and almost as ill-looking.* A TALE OF TWO CITIES BOOK ii, CH. I

A talk took place between Charles Darnay and Mr. Lorry in Tellson's and a letter, delivered as they were talking, nearly ended in tragedy for the former, and actually did for another – in France. A TALE OF TWO CITIES BOOK ii, CH. XXIV

Temple *The cloisterly Temple,* Dickens calls it when Mr. George of BLEAK HOUSE is passing that way, and for all the changes years have brought, for all the vast damage of bombs and fire, and the rebuilding – most beautifully carried out – a benign stillness and quiet still pervade its ancient precincts.

It would be as well to explain briefly that the legal strongholds broadly called 'Inns' are divided into Inns of Court and Inns of Chancery, the first answerable to and under the authority of the Crown, the second under that of the Lord Chancellor (in their original foundation).

The first, Inns of Court, number four: Inner and Middle Temple, Lincoln's and Gray's.

The second, Inns of Chancery, numbered nine. Some parts of the original buildings are still used by lawyers. The nine were: Clifford's Inn, Clement's Inn, Lyon's Inn, Strand Inn, New Inn, Furnival's Inn, Thavies Inn, Staple Inn and Barnard's Inn.

The Inner and Middle Temple, each conducted separately, as from the beginning, are divided by Middle Temple Lane, existing from earliest days and originally ending with stairs to the River. Dickens touches on both as if one, sometimes disparagingly, often with charming incidents, always as if every court and stone were intimately known to him.

Hugh crossed Fleet Street by Temple Bar for the purpose of visiting Sir John Chester, and *plied the knocker of Middle Temple Gate,* only to be regarded suspiciously and told *we don't sell beer here.* BARNABY RUDGE CH. XL

It was at Middle Temple Gate that Mr. Fipps arranged the meeting with Tom Pinch which followed his engagement at the mysterious chambers in Pump Court, *more quiet and more gloomy than the rest.* MARTIN CHUZZLEWIT CH. XXXIX

Adjacent to the Temple Church stands Goldsmith's Buildings, built on the site of the old chambers occupied by Mortimer Lightwood and Eugene Wrayburn. Mr. Boffin consulted Mortimer Lightwood here in connection with his unexpected inheritance. OUR MUTUAL FRIEND BOOK i, CH. VIII

Eugene Wrayburn sees Mr. Dolls here, in one of the latter's usual maudlin conditions, and bribes him to disclose Lizzie Hexam's address. Bradley Headstone rested, *in a doorway with his eyes upon the Temple Gate* waiting and watching for Eugene Wrayburn to come out that he might follow him. *For anything I know he watches at the Temple Gate all night*, said Eugene carelessly. OUR MUTUAL FRIEND BOOK iii, CH. X, XI

Rogue Riderhood, after seeing *Governors Both* (Mortimer Lightwood and Eugene Wrayburn) in the Temple, *pulled his drowned cap over his ears with both hands . . . went down the stairs, round by Temple church, across the Temple, into Whitefriars, and so on by the waterside streets.* OUR MUTUAL FRIEND BOOK i, CH. XII

Garden Court, Temple

Having been to Miss Havisham's, Pip returned to London. It was past midnight when he crossed London Bridge and choosing Whitefriars Gate, the Temple being closed, the night porter handed him a note in Wemmick's hand: *Don't go home.* GREAT EXPECTATIONS CH. XLIV

Pip says *Our Chambers were in Garden Court, down by the river. . . . Alterations have been made in that part of the Temple since that time, and it has not now so lonely a character as it had then, nor is it exposed to the river. We lived at the top of the last house, and the wind rushing up the river shook the house that night. . . .* Here Magwitch revealed himself as the source of Pip's 'Great Expectations'. GREAT EXPECTATIONS CH. XXXIX

The morning after Provis (alias Magwitch) had made himself known to Pip, the latter, groping for a light, went down to the Porter's Lodge for one and stumbled on a crouching figure, which had gone by the time he returned – with the watchman. Questioning the latter as to who had called at the Lodge the night before, the watchman accounted for three, two of whom *lived in the Lane* (Temple Lane). This episode heightened Pip's fears for the safety of the convict Magwitch. GREAT EXPECTATIONS CH. XL

When all was over and Magwitch, fatally injured in his attempt to leave the country with Pip, having died mercifully before his execution, Pip became very ill. On recovering consciousness he found the ever faithful Joe Gargery by him. In due course Joe had a carriage brought into the Lane, wrapped Pip in blankets and carried him over to it. GREAT EXPECTATIONS CH. LVII

Sir John Chester had Chambers in Paper Buildings: *A row of goodly tenements, shaded in front by ancient trees and looking at the back upon Temple Gardens.* Here, earlier, Hugh visited him. After the Gordon riots had been quelled and judgment passed on, among others, Hugh, Dennis and Barnaby, Sir John, in bed in those same Chambers in Paper Buildings, cynically commented on the fate of those three, so convenient to himself, enjoying the *bright, morning sun,* as he partook delicately of his breakfast. The original Paper Buildings were destroyed by fire in 1838. BARNABY RUDGE CH. XV, LXXV

Sydney Carton *turned into the Temple, and, having revived himself by twice pacing the pavement of King's Bench Walk and Paper Buildings, turned into Stryver's Chambers,* to work late for Stryver who owed much to this brilliant, unhappy man. A TALE OF TWO CITIES BOOK ii, CH. V

King's Bench Walk leads down to the river, and the site of Temple Stairs to the west, at the bottom of Middle Temple Lane. Here Mr. Tarter kept his boat and rowed Rosa up the river, with Mr. Grewgious. Here, too, Pip kept the boat which he used in his exploit with Herbert on behalf of Magwitch. EDWIN DROOD CH. XXII; GREAT EXPECTATIONS CH. XLVI

There are still worse places than the Temple on a sultry day, for basking in the sun or resting idly in the shade. There is yet a drowsiness in its Courts and a dreamy dullness in its trees and gardens; those who pace its lanes and squares may yet hear the echoes of their footsteps on the sounding stones, and read upon its gates 'Who enters here leaves noise behind'. BARNABY RUDGE CH. XV

In Fountain Court, *There is still the plash of falling water.* Dickens wove a romance round this Court involving Ruth Pinch, her brother Tom and John Westlock. *There was a little plot between them* (Ruth and Tom) *that Tom should always come out of the Temple by one way and that was past the fountain. Coming through Fountain Court he was just to glance down the steps leading into Garden Court and to look once all round him; and if Ruth had come he would see her. . . . Either she was a little too soon, or Tom was a little too late . . . but no Tom was there. . . . But was anybody else there, that she blushed so deeply . . . ? Why, the fact is that Mr. Westlock was passing at that moment. . . . Merrily the tiny fountain played, and merrily the dimples sparkled on its sunny face. John Westlock hurried after her. Softly the whispering water broke and fell . . . 'I felt sure it was you',* said John, when he overtook her, in the *sanctuary of Garden Court. . . . She was so surprised. . . .* MARTIN CHUZZLEWIT CH. XLV

On another occasion, *Brilliantly the Temple Fountain sparkled in the sun, and laughingly its liquid music played . . . as little Ruth and her companion came towards it. . . . And why they came towards the Fountain at all is a mystery; . . . It was not in their way. . . . Oh wicked little Ruth!* The whole chapter is a delight. MARTIN CHUZZLEWIT CH. LIII

Temple Bar The 'Griffin' divides Fleet Street from the Strand, on the site where the bar once stood. Temple Bar now stands at the entrance to Theobald's Park, Cheshunt.

That leaden-headed old obstruction, appropriate ornament for the threshold of a leaden-headed old corporation: Temple Bar. And on the hottest day in the long vacation, *Temple Bar gets so hot, that it is, to the adjacent Strand and Fleet Street, what a heater is in an urn, and keeps them simmering all night.* BLEAK HOUSE CH. I, XIX

The 'Prentice Knights took an oath not an any account *to damage or in any way disfigure Temple Bar, which was strictly constitutional, and always to be approached with reverence.* BARNABY RUDGE CH. VIII

Temple Bar was headless and forlorn in those degenerate days when Mr. Dorrit passed under it. LITTLE DORRIT BOOK ii, CH. XVII

David Copperfield and Dan'l Peggotty came *through Temple Bar into the City,* with the purpose of finding Martha and enlisting her help in the search for little Em'ly. DAVID COPPERFIELD CH. XLVI

Tom Pinch stepped inside Temple Bar itself to laugh heartily over the beef steak pudding made with flour and eggs, until John Westlock and his sister fairly ran away from him and left him to have his laugh out by himself. MARTIN CHUZZLEWIT CH. XLV

Tenterden Street See Hanover Square.

Thames Betsey Trotwood *was quite gracious on the subject of the Thames (it really did look very well with the sun upon it, though not like the sea before the cottage).* DAVID COPPERFIELD CH. XXXV

We grant the banks of the Thames are very beautiful at Richmond and Twickenham. SKETCHES BY BOZ: THE RIVER

The Thames figures in the attempt of Pip to get his benefactor safely aboard the Continental-bound steamer in the reaches below Gravesend, and there is a wonderfully detailed description of the navigation necessary. Dickens actually took a journey by steamer to try it out. GREAT EXPECTATIONS CH. LIV

Thames Street Known in Dickens's day simply as Thames Street, not 'Upper' or 'Lower' as today.

The Vintner, whose account Joe Willet had to settle on his visit to London, had his place of business *down in some deep cellars hard by Thames Street.* BARNABY RUDGE CH. XIII

Simon Tappertit was taking a lock *to be fitted on a 'ware-us' door in Thames Street,* when he stopped in the Temple to speak with Sir John Chester, who requested him to remove the offending oily smelling lock outside the door. BARNABY RUDGE CH. XXIV

See Custom House.

Thavies Inn (gone as a result of bombing). Mrs. Jellyby's, where Esther, Ada and Richard were to lodge, was *no distance* from Kenge & Carboy's said Mr. Guppy, *round in Thavies Inn . . . only round the corner. We just twist up Chancery Lane, and cut along Holborn, and there we are in four minutes' time as near as a toucher.* So, says Esther Summerson *we turned up under an archway to our destination: a narrow street of high houses, like an oblong cistern to hold the fog. There was a confused little crowd of people, principally children, gathered about the house at which we stopped, which had a tarnished brass plate on the door, with the inscription 'Jellyby'. 'Don't be frightened', said Mr. Guppy, looking in at the coach window, 'One of the young Jellyby's been and got his head through the area railings!'* BLEAK HOUSE CH. IV

Threadneedle Street The Flower Pot Inn, Bishopsgate Street, stood until 1863 at the corner of Threadneedle Street. From here Mr. Minns took a coach to his cousin's at Poplar Walk. SKETCHES BY BOZ: MR. MINNS AND HIS COUSIN

Titbull's Almshouses There seems no doubt that the Vintner's Almshouses, in the Mile End Road, were the original of Titbull's Almshouses *. . . in the east of London, in a great highway, in a poor, busy and thronged neighbourhood. Old iron, and fried fish, cough drops and artificial flowers, boiled pigs-feet and household furniture that looks as if it were polished up with lip-salve, umbrellas full of vocal literature and saucers full of shell-fish in a green juice which I hope is natural to them when their health is good, garnish the paved sideways as you go to Titbull's. I take the ground to have risen in those parts since Titbull's time,*

and you drop into his domain by three stone steps. UNCOMMERCIAL
TRAVELLER: TITBULL'S ALMSHOUSES

Took's Court, EC4. The original of Cook's Court, where
Mr. Snagsby, law stationer, pursues his lawful calling. BLEAK
HOUSE CH. X

Tooley Street The Borough Clink in Tooley Street was one
of the places where *six and thirty fires were raging* at one time
during the Gordon riots. BARNABY RUDGE CH. LXVII

Tooting Snagsby's maid Guster, *was farmed, or contracted for,
during her growing time, by an amiable benefactor of his species
resident in Tooting.* BLEAK HOUSE CH. X
    *When . . . a fatal epidemic had broken out in Mr. Drouet's
farming establishment for pauper children at Tooting, the comfortable
flourish of trumpets usual on such occasions* decided that *of all
similar establishments on earth, that at Tooting was the most
admirable. . . . The learned coroner . . . deemed it quite unnecessary
to hold any inquests on these dead children. We will refer to a very
different kind of coroner, Mr. Wakeley.* His way was to *institute
a very searching inquiry into the causes of these horrors . . . it then
comes out – truth is so perverse – that Mr. Drouet is not altogether
that golden farmer he is supposed to be.* (An instance of Dickens's
social conscience, expressed in strongly written, scathing
words, that so often helped to right wrongs.) MISCELLANEOUS
PAPERS: THE PARADISE AT TOOTING

Tottenham Court Road In this road were the cheap linen
drapers, Messrs. Jones, Spruggins and Smith. Here the true
identity of Horatio Sparkins was discovered by Mrs.
Malderton and her daughters. SKETCHES BY BOZ: HORATIO
SPARKINS
    It was at the broker's shop *at the top of Tottenham Court
Road,* that *the little round table with the marble top, and Sophy's
flower-pot and stand* belonging to Traddles and seized by the
broker when the Micawber household in Camden Town
was sold up, were recovered by the aid of Clara Peggotty.
DAVID COPPERFIELD CH. XXXIV

Miss Knag's brother, *an ornamental stationer and small circulating library keeper*, lived *in a by-street off Tottenham Court Road; and who let out by the day, week, month or year, the newest old novels, whereof the titles were displayed in pen-and-ink characters on a sheet of pasteboard, swinging at his door post.* NICHOLAS NICKLEBY CH. XVIII

Dickens used to come this way as a boy from his home in Gower Street to the Blacking factory at Charing Cross – *I could not resist the stale pastry put out at half price on trays at the confectioners' doors in Tottenham Court Road.* LIFE

We never recollect to have been more amused with a hackney coach party, than one we saw early the other morning in Tottenham Court Road. It was a wedding-party, and emerged from one of the inferior streets near Fitzroy Square. There were the bride, with a thin white dress and a great red face; and the bridesmaid, a little, dumpy, good-humoured young woman, dressed, of course, in the same appropriate costume; and the bridegroom and his chosen friend, in blue coats, yellow waistcoats, white trousers, and Berlin gloves to match. They stopped at the corner of the street, and called a coach with an air of indescribable dignity. The moment they were in, the bridesmaid threw a red shawl, which she had, no doubt, brought on purpose, negligently over the number on the door, evidently to delude pedestrians into the belief that the hackney-coach was a private carriage; and away they went, perfectly satisfied that the imposition was successful, and quite unconscious that there was a great staring number stuck up behind on a plate as large as a schoolboy's slate. A shilling a mile! – the ride was worth five at least, to them. SKETCHES BY BOZ: HACKNEY COACH STANDS

The Tower of London and **Tower Hill** It was at the garden up by Trinity House on Tower Hill that Bella Wilfer waited, while Pa bought himself *the most beautiful suit of clothes, the most beautiful hat and the most beautiful pair of bright boots,* for the purpose of their *innocent elopement* to Greenwich. OUR MUTUAL FRIEND BOOK ii, CH. VIII

Quilp resided on Tower Hill and in her bower on Tower Hill, Mrs. Quilp was left to pine the absence of her lord when he quitted her on business. No. 2 Tower Hill, now gone, is said to have been the house in question. OLD CURIOSITY SHOP CH. IV

In Tower Street formerly stood The Crooked Billet, headquarters of the recruiting Serjeant from whom Joe Willet took the King's shilling. BARNABY RUDGE CH. XXXI

In the early stages of the Gordon riots, Simon Tappertit went back one night to the house of Gabriel Varden, his master. Taking in the dishevelled and drunken state of his apprentice, and having his fears confirmed as to his share in the riots, Gabriel yet showed his humanity and warning him of the peril he stood in and turning to his now frightened wife, proposed that Simon should get a couple of hours sleep, wash and change his dress, so that he *might get to the Tower Stairs, and away by the Gravesend tide boat, before a search is made for him.* From there he could get to Canterbury

Tower of London

where Mrs. Varden's cousin might *give him work till this storm has blown over.* Simon Tappertit, needless to say, took no warning and fled from his generous master to more mischief. BARNABY RUDGE CH. LI

In the Tower of London, *in a dreary room whose thick stone walls shut out the hum of life, and made a stillness which the records left by former prisoners . . . seemed to deepen and intensify; remorseful for every act that had been done by every man among the cruel crowd; feeling for the time their guilt his own and . . . little comfort in fanaticism . . . sat the unhappy author of all – Lord George Gordon!* BARNABY RUDGE CH. LXXIII

David Copperfield as a boy used to meet the 'Orfling' on London Bridge, there to tell her *some astonishing fictions respecting the wharves and the Tower; of which I say no more than I hope I believed them myself.* DAVID COPPERFIELD CH. XI

When managing Clara Peggotty's affairs David varied *the legal character of these proceedings by going to see . . . the Tower of London.* DAVID COPPERFIELD CH. XXXIII

Trinity House See Tower of London.

Turnham Green *That magnificent potentate, the Lord Mayor of London, was made to stand and deliver on Turnham Green by one highwayman, who despoiled the illustrious creature in sight of all his retinue.* This and such instances were cited to show that in England, even, things were not much better in respect of order, than in Paris where a Revolution was boiling up. A TALE OF TWO CITIES BOOK i, CH. I

Turnstile Mr. Snagsby would tell his two apprentices *how he has heard say that a brook 'as clear as crystal' once ran right down the middle of Holborn, when Turnstile really was a turnstile, leading slap away into the meadows.* BLEAK HOUSE CH. X

Tyburn Referring to Mr. Dennis's (hangman at Newgate) allusions to the flourishing condition of his trade in those days, Dickens cites the cruel case of Mary Jones (under nineteen and a mother of two) who lived a normal honest life till her husband was pressed into army service on an alarm about the Falkland Islands. Her subsequent complete destitution resulted, she was turned into the streets to beg, took or stole some linen off a counter, and though, when a shopman saw her, she put it down, she was hanged at Tyburn. (A stone near Marble Arch marks the site of the gallows.) BARNABY RUDGE PREFACE.

They hanged at Tyburn, in those days, so the street outside Newgate had not obtained the infamous notoriety that has since attached to it. A TALE OF TWO CITIES BOOK ii, CH. II

Vauxhall Bridge *One evening in October I was walking with Henrietta, enjoying the cool breezes wafted over Vauxhall Bridge.* CHRISTMAS STORIES: SOMEBODY'S LUGGAGE

Bradley Headstone and Charley Hexam, on returning from visiting Hexam's sister, cross Vauxhall Bridge. OUR MUTUAL FRIEND BOOK ii, CH. I

The Sunday water-party goes in the direction of Vauxhall Bridge. SKETCHES BY BOZ: THE RIVER

Vauxhall Gardens Vauxhall station is near the site of Vauxhall Gardens. Boz gives an account of these gardens by day: *a thing hardly to be thought of!* He likens it by daylight to *A porter-pot without porter, the House of Commons without the Speaker, a gas-lamp without the gas.* SKETCHES BY BOZ: VAUXHALL GARDENS BY DAY

Verulam Buildings, Gray's Inn. . . . . *the scowling iron-barred prison-like passage into Verulam Buildings, the mouldy red-nosed ticket porters.* . . . UNCOMMERCIAL TRAVELLER: CHAMBERS

Veterinary Hospital, Royal College Street. Traddles lived in a little street near the Veterinary College at Camden Town. David found he was lodging with the Micawbers. DAVID COPPERFIELD CH. XXVII

Victoria Theatre *The streets in the vicinity of . . . Victoria Theatre present an appearance of dirt and discomfort on such a night,*

*which the groups who lounge about them in no degree tend to diminish.
. . . Here they amuse themselves with theatrical converse, arising out
of their last half-price visit to the Victoria gallery.* This is the
theatre generally known as The Old Vic in the Waterloo
Road. SKETCHES BY BOZ: THE STREETS – NIGHT

   *. . . put Joe in the gallery of the Victoria Theatre . . . tell him
a story . . . and by the help of live men and women dressed up, confiding to him their innermost secrets, in voices audible half a mile
off; and Joe will unravel a story through all its entanglements,
and sit there as long after midnight as you
have anything left to show him. Accordingly,
the Theatres to which Mr. Whelks resorts,
are always full; and whatever changes of
fashion the drama knows elsewhere, it is always
fashionable in the New Cut.* MISCELLANEOUS
PAPERS: AMUSEMENTS OF THE PEOPLE

Walcot Square A little past the Bethlehem Hospital is Kennington Road, off
which is Walcot Square. Mr. Guppy in
proposing to Esther informed her he had
taken *a 'ouse in that locality . . . a hollow
bargain (taxes ridiculous, and use of fixtures
included in rent).* He added, *I beg to lay the
'ouse in Walcot Square, the business and
myself, before Miss Summerson for her acceptance.* BLEAK HOUSE
CH. LXIV

Walworth Wemmick lived in Walworth with his father, in
*a little wooden cottage in the midst of plots of garden, and the top of
it was cut out and painted like a battery mounted with guns. 'My
own doing', said Wemmick, 'looks pretty, don't it?' I highly com-
mended it. I think it was the smallest house I ever saw: with the
queerest gothic windows (by far the greater part of them sham), and
a gothic door, almost too small to get in at. 'That's a real flagstaff,
you see' said Wemmick, 'and on Sundays I run up a real flag. Then
look here. After I have crossed the bridge, I hoist it up – so – and*

cut off the communication'. The bridge was a plank and it crossed a chasm about four feet wide and two deep. But it was very pleasant to see the pride with which he hoisted it up, and made it fast; smiling as he did so. GREAT EXPECTATIONS CH. XXV

I cannot imagine what Walworth has done, to bring such a windy punishment upon itself, as I never fail to find recorded in the newspapers when the wind has blown at all hard. . . . But there can hardly be any Walworth left by this time. UNCOMMERCIAL TRAVELLER: REFRESHMENTS FOR TRAVELLERS

The back part of Walworth, at its greatest distance from town, is a straggling miserable place enough, even in these days; but five-and-thirty years ago, the greater portion of it was little better than a dreary waste, inhabited by a few scattered people of most questionable character, whose poverty prevented their living in any better neighbourhood, or whose pursuits and mode of life rendered its solitude peculiarly desirable. SKETCHES BY BOZ: THE BLACK VEIL

Wapping The rioters were bound for Wapping to destroy a chapel, while other parties left for similar mischief. BARNABY RUDGE CH. LIII

The Uncommercial set out to see for himself the Wapping Workhouse, because of a magistrate's report in a morning paper, *that there was no classification at the Wapping Workhouse for women, and that it was a disgrace and a shame.* UNCOMMERCIAL TRAVELLER: WAPPING WORKHOUSE

Warwick Street, W1. At No. 12 is a Roman Catholic church, no doubt the one referred to in the riots: *The men who are loitering in the streets tonight are half-disposed to pull down a Romish chapel or two . . . they only want leaders. I even heard mention of those in . . . Warwick Street.* Later, Simon Tappertit denies to the Vardens that he was *at Warwick Street*, but he proudly asserts that *he was at Westminster!* BARNABY RUDGE CH. LI

Waterloo Bridge (rebuilt 1939). *Over Waterloo Bridge, there is a shabby old speckled couple* (chickens) *. . . who are always trying to get in at the door of a chapel. Whether the old lady, under a delusion reminding one of Mrs. Southcott, has an idea of entrusting an egg to that particular denomination, or merely understands that she has* *no business in the building and is consequently frantic to enter it, I cannot determine . . . while her partner, who is infirm upon his legs, walks up and down, encouraging her and defying the Universe.* UNCOMMERCIAL TRAVELLER: SHY NEIGHBOURHOODS

Drip, drip, drip, from ledge and coping, splash from pipes and water-spouts, and by-and-by the houseless shadow would fall upon the stones that pave the way to Waterloo Bridge; it being in the houseless mind to have a half-penny worth of excuse for saying 'Goodnight' to the toll-keeper, and catching a glimpse of his fire. A good fire and a good greatcoat and a good woollen neck shawl were comfortable things to see in conjunction with the toll-keeper; also his brisk wakefulness was excellent company when he rattled the change of halfpence down upon that metal table of his, like a man who defied the night, with all its sorrowful thoughts, and didn't care for the coming of dawn . . . the bridge was dreary. UNCOMMERCIAL TRAVELLER: NIGHT WALKS

The drunkard's death, by drowning, which he had sought, then struggled to avoid, began as *He crept softly down the steep stone stairs that lead from the commencement of Waterloo Bridge, down to the water's level.* SKETCHES BY BOZ: THE DRUNKARD'S DEATH

'*Service, sir*', exlaimed Sam. '*You may say that. Arter I ran away from the carrier, and afore I took up with the vagginer, I had unfurnished lodgings for a fortnight. . . . the dry arches of Waterloo Bridge. Fine sleeping place – within ten minutes' walk of all the public offices – only if there is any objection to it, it is that the sitivation's rayther too airy. I see some queer sights there*'. PICKWICK PAPERS CH. XVI

Welbeck Street Lord George Gordon rode *along the Strand, up Swallow Street, into Oxford Road and thence to his house in Welbeck Street, near Cavendish Square, whither he was attended by a few dozen idlers.* His house was No. 64, close to Wigmore Street (since rebuilt). BARNABY RUDGE CH. XXXVII

Well Street (now Ensign Street, E1). Following the footsteps of young Dickens, as narrated in GONE ASTRAY, *I must have strayed by that time, as I recall my course, into Goodman Fields, or somewhere thereabouts. The picture represented a scene in a play then performing at a theatre in that neighbourhood which is no longer*

in existence. It stimulated me to go to that theatre and see that play
. . . I found out the theatre – of its external appearance I only
remember the loyal initials G.R. untidily painted in yellow ochre
on the front. The theatre in Goodman's Fields (where Garrick
made his first London appearance) disappeared in 1802, so
the one Dickens refers to was no doubt that in Well Street
called The Royalty, or East London Theatre, burnt down in
April 1826. The site is now occupied by a Hostel. MISCEL-
LANEOUS PAPERS: GONE ASTRAY

Wellington House Academy See Hampstead Road.

Wellington Street See 'Household Words' and 'All The
Year Round'.

West India Docks *Captain Cuttle lived on the brink of a little*
canal near the India Docks, where there was a swivel bridge which
opened now and then to let some wandering monster of a ship come
roaming up the street like a stranded leviathan. The gradual change
from land to water, on the approach to Captain Cuttle's lodgings, was
curious. It began with the erection of flagstaffs, as appurtenances to
public-houses; then came slopsellers' shops with Guernsey shirts,
sou'wester hats, and canvas pantaloons, at once the tightest and
loosest of their order, hanging up outside. These were succeeded by
anchors and chain-cable forges, where sledge-hammers were dinging
upon iron all day long. Then came rows of houses, with little vane-
surmounted masts uprearing themselves from among the scarlet
beans. Then ditches. Then pollard willows. Then more ditches. Then
unaccountable patches of dirty water, hardly to be descried, for the
ships that covered them. Then the air was perfumed with chips;
and all other trades were swallowed up in mast, oar and blockmaking,
and boat-building. Then, the ground grew marshy and unsettled.
Then, there was nothing to be smelt but rum and sugar. Then Captain
Cuttle's lodgings – at once a first floor and a top story, in Brig
Place – were close before you. It has been suggested that Brig
Place could have been the cul-de-sac that once lay by the
City Arms on the Limehouse side of the City Canal – now
South West India Docks. The boy Charles Dickens went
frequently to see his godfather, Christopher Huffam, living

at 5 Church Street, whence he could have walked by Three Colt and Emmett Streets to Bridge Road and so the Dock, quite a short walk from his godfather's. DOMBEY AND SON CH. IX, XV; THE DICKENSIAN: SUMMER 1935

Westminster Abbey Here the body of Charles Dickens is enshrined. The stone placed upon the grave is inscribed:

CHARLES DICKENS

BORN FEBRUARY THE SEVENTH, 1812

DIED JUNE THE NINTH, 1870

Facing the grave, on its left and right, are the monuments of Chaucer, Shakespeare and Dryden, *the three immortals who did most to create and settle the language to which Charles Dickens has given another undying name.* LIFE

A somewhat prophetic reference is made in LITTLE DORRIT: *Time shall show us. The post of honour and the post of shame . . . a peer's statue in Westminster Abbey, and a seaman's hammock in the bosom of the deep . . . only Time shall show us whither each traveller is bound.* LITTLE DORRIT BOOK i, CH. XV

In reference to Miss Abbey Potterson: *Some waterside heads . . . harboured muddled notions that, because of her dignity and firmness,* Miss Abbey Potterson who kept the Six Jolly Fellowship Porters at Limehouse, *was named after, or in some way related to, the Abbey at Westminster.* OUR MUTUAL FRIEND BOOK i, CH. VI

Pip and Herbert went to a morning service at Westminster Abbey, and in the afternoon walked in the parks, when Pip wondered who shod all the horses, and wished Joe did! GREAT EXPECTATIONS CH. XXII

When David Copperfield and Dan'l Peggotty, in the hope of news of Little Em'ly, followed Martha from Blackfriars to Millbank, *Westminster Abbey was the point at which she passed from the lights and noise of the leading streets.* DAVID COPPERFIELD CH. XLVII

Westminster Bridge *I was on Westminster Bridge, regaling my houseless eyes with the external walls of the British Parliament — the perfection of a stupendous institution, I know, and the admiration*

of all surrounding nations and succeeding ages, I do not doubt, but perhaps a little the better now and then for being pricked up to its work. UNCOMMERCIAL TRAVELLER: NIGHT WALKS

The Pickwickians went over Westminster Bridge to Rochester from the Golden Cross at Charing Cross in 1827. PICKWICK PAPERS CH. II

Mr. Peggotty on his first return to London after his search for Little Em'ly found *a traveller's lodging on the Dover Road,* and David accompanied him over Westminster Bridge and parted from him on the Surrey side. DAVID COPPERFIELD CH. XL

Barnaby, after enlisting under the leadership of Lord George Gordon on the bridge, crossed it with him and went down Bridge Road to join the throng at St. George's Fields. BARNABY RUDGE CH. XLVII, XLVIII, XLIX

Miss Morleena Kenwigs had received an invitation to repair next day per steamer from Westminster Bridge, unto the Eel-pie Island at Twickenham: there to make merry upon a cold collation, bottled-beer, shrub and shrimps. . . . NICHOLAS NICKLEBY CH. LII

It is interesting to note how the river in Dickens's day was looked on as a speedier mode of transportation than merely roads, whether by using boats or crossing and re-crossing certain bridges to cut time. As an instance, Riah, the Jew from St. Mary Axe, wanting to visit Jenny Wren, the little Doll's dressmaker, *passed over London Bridge, and returned to the Middlesex shore by that of Westminster, and so, ever wading through the fog, waded to the doorstep of the Doll's dressmaker.* (In Smith Square.) OUR MUTUAL FRIEND BOOK iii, CH. II

Bradley Headstone and Charley Hexam crossed Westminster Bridge on their way to see Hexam's sister. OUR MUTUAL FRIEND BOOK ii, CH. I

The Sunday water-party *proceeds towards Westminster Bridge, amidst such a splashing and struggling as never was seen before. . . .* SKETCHES BY BOZ: THE RIVER

Westminster Hall In the Preface of the PICKWICK PAPERS, Dickens tells us how when his first literary effusion *appeared in all the glory of print,* he *walked down to Westminster Hall and turned into it for half-an-hour because my eyes were so dimmed with*

joy and pride that they could not bear the street, and were not fit to be seen there.

One of the dozen or so places where parties of soldiers were posted on guard against the Gordon rioters was Palace Yard, outside Westminster Hall. BARNABY RUDGE CH. LXVII

See Palace Yard.

In a building to the north of the Old Hall the Law Courts were held until 1883, when the new buildings in Fleet Street were opened, and here the final scenes in the cause *célèbre* Jarndyce *v.* Jarndyce, were enacted. The opening scenes in BLEAK HOUSE dealing with this case were, of course, at Lincoln's Inn Hall. (See Lincoln's Inn.) BLEAK HOUSE CH. LXV

Lord George Gordon, remaining in his prison in the Tower until Monday, the fifth day of February in the following year, after the riots were over, was on that day solemnly tried at Westminster for High Treason. *Of this crime, he was, after a patient investigation, declared Not Guilty; upon the ground that there was no proof of his having called the multitude together with any traitorous or unlawful intentions.* BARNABY RUDGE CH. LXXXII

During the long vacation when *the public offices lie in a hot sleep; Westminster Hall itself is a shady solitude where nightingales might sing, and a tenderer class of suitors than is usually found there, walk.* BLEAK HOUSE CH. XIX

Bar (a name given by Dickens to the legal world) *knew all about the gullibility and knavery of people; but Physician* (the medical world) *could have given him a better insight into their tendernesses and affections, in one week of his rounds, than Westminster Hall and all the circuits put together, in threescore years and ten.* LITTLE DORRIT BOOK ii, CH. XXV

Whitechapel Lord George Gordon, after leaving the Maypole Inn where he had stayed the night, rode *the whole length of Whitechapel, Leadenhall Street, Cheapside into St. Paul's Churchyard.* BARNABY RUDGE CH. XXXVII

At the Black Lion Inn – parts of the yard are still to be seen at No. 75 Whitechapel Road – Joe Willet had his meals ordered for him and was recommended by his father not to score up too large a bill there. BARNABY RUDGE CH. XIII

Sam remarked, *Not a wery nice neighbourhood this, . . . It's a wery remarkable circumstance, sir, that poverty and oysters always seems to go together. . . . Look here, sir; here's a oyster stall to every half dozen houses. The streets lined vith 'em. Blessed if I don't think that ven a man's wery poor, he rushes out of his lodgings, and eats oysters in reg'lar desperation.* PICKWICK PAPERS CH. XXII

The house where Oliver had been taken, in preparation for the burglary at Chertsey, was in the neighbourhood of Whitechapel. OLIVER TWIST CH. XIX

Whitechapel Church *I had got past Whitechapel Church and was rather inappropriately for an Uncommercial Traveller – in the Commercial Road.* UNCOMMERCIAL TRAVELLER: WAPPING WORKHOUSE

Whitechapel Workhouse *On the fifth of last November, I, the Conductor of this journal accompanied by a friend . . . accidentally strayed into Whitechapel . . . when we found ourselves at eight o'clock before the Workhouse.* MISCELLANEOUS PAPERS: A NIGHTLY SCENE IN LONDON

White Conduit House The May Day celebrations among sweeps were declining and an anniversary dinner at White Conduit House was substituted – *where clean faces appeared in lieu of black ones smeared with rose pink.* SKETCHES BY BOZ: FIRST OF MAY

Grimaldi the clown, whose memoirs Dickens edited, lies buried in a churchyard in this area. He lived at 37 Penton Street, where the White Conduit formerly stood.

Whitecross Street The threat of Whitecross Street (a notorious Debtors' Prison) had a terrifying effect upon the 'young gentleman' held prisoner in Namby's office. The prison was demolished 1865–70. PICKWICK PAPERS CH. XL

Whitefriars Mr. Jerry Cruncher's private lodging was in Hanging Sword Alley, Whitefriars. A TALE OF TWO CITIES BOOK ii, CH. I

At the back of Fleet Street, and lying between it and the water-side, are several mean and narrow courts, which form a portion of White-friars. . . . SKETCHES BY BOZ: THE DRUNKARD'S DEATH
See Temple.

Whitehall Passing the old Palace of Whitehall caused Mr. Jingle to remark, *Looking at Whitehall, sir – fine place – little window – somebody else's head off there, eh, sir?* referring to his own recent remark as they passed in their coach under the archway of the Golden Cross Hotel. PICKWICK PAPERS CH. II
   The Home Office, Whitehall, was one of the avenues through which *Old John's* patent took its unlucky course – to failure. REPRINTED PIECES: A POOR MAN'S TALE OF A PATENT

Whitehall Place See Scotland Yard.

White Hart Inn See Borough.

White Horse Cellars See Piccadilly.

Wimpole Street See Harley Street.

Windsor Terrace See City Road.

Wine Office Court At No. 146 Fleet Street is Wine Office Court, in which that famous tavern, the Cheshire Cheese, is to be found. Although never mentioned by name, so famous an Inn, with its associations with Dr. Johnson, must have been well known to Dickens. It is thought probable that he had the Cheshire Cheese in mind when Sydney Carton induced Charles Darnay to dine with him, after the latter's acquittal at the Old Bailey of the charge of High Treason. They went *down Ludgate Hill to Fleet Street, and so up a covered way into a tavern.* A TALE OF TWO CITIES BOOK ii, CH. IV

Woburn Place *We were to make for Chigwell . . . and to start from the residence of the projectors, Woburn Place, Russell Square.* SKETCHES OF YOUNG GENTLEMEN: THE YOUNG LADIES' YOUNG GENTLEMAN

Wood Street Mr. Mould, the undertaker, lived hereabouts: *Deep in the City, and within the Ward of Cheap, stood Mr. Mould's establishment . . . abutting on a churchyard small and shady.* His premises were in a quiet corner, *where the City strife became a drowsy hum . . . suggesting to a thoughtful mind a stoppage in Cheapside.* MARTIN CHUZZLEWIT CH. XXV

See Cross Keys Inn.

Wyldes Farm See Hampstead (illustration on page 72).

How to get there

Many of the places mentioned in the text are
famous London landmarks, as well known today
as they were in Dickens's lifetime. These are
included in London Transport's booklet
How to get There, *from which the details below
are taken.* How to get There *lists hundreds of
places of interest in the London area, on sale at London
Transport Travel Information Centres, from most
Underground station booking offices, or post free from the
Publicity Office Shop,* 280 *Old Marylebone Road,
London* NW1.

London's bus services are undergoing a major
reorganization and details included here are liable
to alteration. Before visiting any of these places,
or if you wish to visit some of the other sites
associated with Dickens, it may be advisable to
check your route by ringing
01–222 1234 *at any time, day or night.*

Adelphi Theatre
Strand, WC2
Underground: Charing Cross
Bus: 1, 6, 9, 11, 13, 15, 77, 77A, 77C, 176

Albany Piccadilly, W1
Underground: Piccadilly Circus
Bus: 3, 6, 9, 12, 13, 14, 15, 19, 22, 38,
53, 88, 159

All Souls' Church
Langham Place, Regent Street, W1
Underground: Oxford Circus
Bus: 1, 3, 6, 7, 8, 12, 13, 15, 25, 39, 53,
73, 88, 113, 137, 159, 500

Bank of England
Threadneedle Street, EC2
Underground: Bank, Monument
Bus: 6, 8, 11, 15, 21, 22, 23, 25, 43, 76,
133, 149, 501, 502

**Bethlehem Hospital,
now Imperial War Museum**
Lambeth Road, SE1
Mons. to Sats. 1000 to 1750
Suns. 1400 to 1750
Closed New Year's Day, Good Fri.,
5 May, Christmas Eve and Day, Boxing
Day
Underground: Lambeth North,
Elephant & Castle
Bus: 1, 3, 10, 12, 44, 45, 53, 63, 109, 141,
155, 159, 171, 172, 176, 184, 188

Blackheath, SE3
Bus: 53, 54, 75, 89, 108, 108B, 192

Bloomsbury
BEDFORD SQUARE
Underground: Tottenham Court Road
Bus: 1, 7, 8, 14, 19, 24, 25, 29, 38, 73,
176

BLOOMSBURY SQUARE
Underground: Holborn
Bus: 5, 7, 8, 19, 22, 25, 38, 55, 68,
77, 77A, 77C, 170, 172, 188, 239
RUSSELL SQUARE
Underground: Russell Square
Bus: 68, 77, 77A, 77C, 170, 239

Bond Street
(Old and New Bond Streets), W1
Underground: Bond Street, Green Park
Bus: 1, 6, 7, 8, 9, 12, 13, 14, 15, 19, 22,
25, 38, 73, 88, 113, 137, 159, 500

British Museum
Great Russell Street, WC1
Mons. to Sats. 1000 to 1700
Suns. 1430 to 1800
Closed New Year's Day, Good Fri.,
5 May, Christmas Eve and Day,
Boxing Day
Underground: Tottenham Court Road,
Goodge Street, Russell Square,
Holborn
Bus: 68, 77, 77A, 77C, 170, 239
to Southampton Row (Great Russell
Street); 7, 8, 19, 22, 25, 38 to New
Oxford Street (Museum Street); 14, 24,
29, 73, 176 to Great Russell Street:
172 to Southampton Place

Buckingham Palace, The Mall, SW1
Underground: St. James's Park, Victoria,
Hyde Park Corner, Green Park
Bus: 2, 2B, 9, 10, 11, 14, 16, 16A, 19,
22, 24, 25, 29, 30, 36, 36A, 36B, 38, 39,
52, 73, 74, 76, 137, 149, 185, 500, 503,
507

**Covent Garden
and Theatre Royal**
Underground: Covent Garden (not Suns.)
Bus: 1, 6, 9, 11, 13, 15, 77, 77A, 77C,
170, 176

Dickens House
48 Doughty Street, WC1
Mons. to Sats. 1000 to 1700
Admission 60p, students 50p, children
25p. Closed New Year's Day, Good Fri.
to Easter Mon., 5 May, Spring and Late
Summer Hol. Mons. and a week at
Christmas
Underground: Russell Square
Bus: 19, 38, 55, 172 to Gray's Inn Road
or 18, 45, 46 to Guilford Street
(Charges under review)

Drury Lane Theatre Royal
Underground: Covent Garden (*not Suns.*),
Holborn, Temple (*not Suns.*)

Bus: 1, 4, 6, 9, 11, 13, 15, 55, 68, 77,
77A, 77C, 168, 170, 171, 172, 176, 188,
239, 502, 513

Duke of York's Column
The Mall, SW1
Underground: Charing Cross
Piccadilly Circus
Bus: 1, 3, 6, 9, 11, 12, 13, 15, 24, 29, 77,
77A, 77C, 88, 168, 170, 176

George Inn
Borough High Street, SE1
Underground: London Bridge
Bus: 8A, 10, 18, 21, 35, 40, 43, 44, 47,
48, 70, 95, 133, 501, 513

Gray's Inn, WC1
Hall, Chapel and Library:
to view, write to the
Under Treasurer
Gardens: May, June, July,
Mons. to Fris. 1200 to 1400:
Aug. and Sept., Mons. to Fris. 0930 to
1700. Closed 24 Dec. to 1 Jan., Good Fri.
to 9 April
Underground: Chancery Lane (*not Suns.*)
Bus: 8, 18, 19, 22, 25, 38, 45, 55, 170,
171, 172, 501

Great Ormond Street Hospital, WC1
Underground: Russell Square
Bus: 18, 45, 68, 77, 77A, 77C, 170, 188,
239

Green Park, SW1
Underground: Green Park
Bus: 2, 2B, 9, 14, 16, 16A, 19, 22, 25,
30, 36, 36B, 38, 52, 73, 74, 137, 500

Greenwich, SE10
Underground: Surrey Docks then bus
108B, 188
Bus: 54, 75, 177, 180, 185

Grosvenor Square, W1
Underground: Bond Street, Marble Arch
Bus: 1, 6, 7, 8, 12, 13, 15, 73, 88, 113,
137, 159, 500, 616 to Oxford St.,
Selfridges; 2, 2B, 16, 16A, 30, 36, 36B,
73, 74, 137 to Grosvenor Gate; 25 to
Brook Street

Guildhall
Corporation of London,
King Street, EC2
Great Hall: Daily 1000 to 1700;
closed Suns. Oct. to Apr. New Year's
Day, Good Fri., Easter weekend and
Mon., Christmas Eve and Day, Boxing
Day and certain other days for official

functions
Underground: Bank, Mansion House
Bus: 6, 8, 9, 11, 15, 21, 22, 23, 25, 43, 76,
133, 501, 502, 513

Guy's Hospital
St. Thomas's Street, SE1
Underground: London Bridge
Bus: 8A, 10, 18, 21, 35, 40, 43, 44, 47,
48, 70, 95, 133, 501, 513

Ham House
near Richmond, Surrey
House: from Apr. to Sept., Tues. to
Suns. 1400 to 1800. Oct. to Mar.,
Tues. to Suns. 1200 to 1600
Closed New Year's Day, Good Fri.,
5 May, Christmas Eve and Day, Boxing
Day
Admission 40p, children 15p
(Charges under review)
Grounds: open daily free
Underground: Richmond then bus 65, 71

Hampstead Heath, NW3
Underground: Hampstead, Golders Green
Bus: 24, 46, 187, 210, 268, C11

Highgate Village
Underground: Archway, Highgate
Bus: 143, 210, 271

Haymarket Theatre Royal
Haymarket, SW1
Underground: Piccadilly Circus
Bus: 3, 6, 9, 12, 13, 14, 15, 19, 22, 38,
53, 88, 159

Horse Guards, Whitehall, SW1
Underground: Charing Cross
Bus: 3, 11, 12, 24, 29, 39, 53, 77, 77A,
77C, 88, 159, 168, 170

Houses of Parliament
Parliament Square, SW1
Conducted tours from 1000 to
1630 on Sats. Also on Bank Hols.,
Mons., Tues. and Thurs. in Aug. and
Thurs. in Sept. if neither house is
sitting
During sessions: admission to the
Strangers' Gallery in the Lords by
arrangement with a peer or MP, or by
queue at St. Stephen's entrance.
Commons Strangers' Gallery by
application to an MP
WESTMINSTER HALL
When Parliament is in session:
Mons. to Thurs. from 1000 to 1330
(if neither House is sitting at the time)
Sat. 1000 to 1700

During recess: Mons. to Fris. from
1000 to 1600, Sat. 1000 to 1700
Closed Good Fri., Christmas Day,
Boxing Day
Underground: Westminster
Bus: 3, 11, 12, 24, 29, 53, 76, 77, 77A,
77C, 88, 109, 155, 159, 168, 170, 172,
184, 503

Hyde Park, W2
Underground: Marble Arch,
Hyde Park Corner,
Lancaster Gate, Knightsbridge
Bus: 2, 2B, 6, 7, 8, 9, 12, 14, 15, 16, 16A,
19, 22, 25, 30, 36, 36B, 38, 52, 73, 74,
88, 137, 500

Kenwood House
Hampstead Lane, NW3
Daily (except Good Fri., Christmas
Eve and Day) 1000 to 1900.
Closes 1700 Oct., Feb., Mar.;
1000 Nov. to Jan. Free
Underground: Archway or
Golders Green then bus 210

Leadenhall Market
Gracechurch Street, EC3
Underground: Bank, Monument
Bus: 8A, 10, 15, 25, 35, 40, 47, 48

Lincoln's Inn
Chancery Lane, WC2
HALLS AND LIBRARY
Admission by prior written permission
only
Chapel and Gardens: Mons. to Fris.
1200 to 1430
Closed New Year's Day, Good Fri.,
Easter weekend and Mon., 5 May,
Spring and Late Summer Hol. Mons.,
Christmas Eve and Day, Boxing Day
Underground: Chancery Lane (*not Suns.*)
Bus: 8, 22, 25, 171, 501

Lincoln's Inn Fields, WC2
Underground: Holborn
Bus: 8, 22, 25, 68, 77, 77A, 77C, 170,
172, 188, 239, 501

London Bridge
see *Guy's Hospital*

London Hospital
Whitechapel Road, E1
Underground: Whitechapel
Bus: 10, 25, 253

Mansion House
Mansion House Street, EC4
Admission to organized parties only

on Tues., Weds. and Thurs. at 1100 and
1400 on prior application to Sec. of
Lord Mayor
No visits end July to mid Sept.
Underground: Bank, Monument
Bus: 6, 8, 9, 11, 15, 21, 22, 25, 43, 76,
133, 149, 501, 502, 513

Marylebone High Street
Underground: Baker Street, Regent's
Park
Bus: 1, 18, 27, 30, 176

Monument
Fish Street Hill, EC3
Mons. to Sats. from Apr. to Sept.
0900 to 1740; Oct. to Mar.
0900 to 1540, on Suns. from
May to Sept. 1400 to 1740
Closed New Year's Day, Good Fri.,
Christmas Day, Boxing Day
Admission 20p, children 10p
(Charges under review)
Underground: Monument
Bus: 8A, 9, 10, 21, 35, 40, 43, 44, 47, 48,
95, 133, 501, 513

Obelisk, Lambeth Road
see *Bethlehem Hospital*

Old Bailey
(Central Criminal Court)
Old Bailey, EC4
The public are admitted when the
Courts are sitting.
Underground: St. Paul's
Bus: 4, 6, 8, 9, 11, 15, 18, 22, 23, 25, 141,
501, 502, 513

Old Curiosity Shop
Portsmouth Street, Kingsway, WC2
Daily except Christmas Day 0900 to
1750
Underground: Holborn
Bus: 55, 68, 77, 77A, 77C, 170, 172, 188,
239

Old Vic, Waterloo Road, SE1
Underground: Waterloo
Bus: 1, 4, 68, 70, 76, 176, 188, 239, 501,
502, 513

Putney
Underground: Putney Bridge, East Putney
Bus: 14, 30, 37, 39, 74, 85, 85A, 93

Regent's Park, NW1
Underground: Baker Street,
Regent's Park, Great Portland Street,
Camden Town

Bus: 1, 2, 2B, 3, 13, 18, 27, 30, 53, 74,
113, 137, 159, 176

Richmond-upon-Thames
Underground: Richmond
Bus: 27, 33, 37, 65, 71, 73, 90, 90B, 202,
270, 290

Roman Bath
5 Strand Lane, WC2
Underground: Temple (*not Suns.*)
Bus: 1, 4, 6, 9, 11, 13, 15, 55, 68, 77,
77A, 77C, 109, 155, 168, 170, 171, 172,
176, 184, 188, 239, 502, 513

Royal Exchange, Cornhill, EC3
see *Bank of England*

Sadler's Wells Theatre
Rosebery Avenue, EC1
Underground: Angel
Bus: 19, 38, 171, 172, 279

St. Bartholomew's Hospital
West Smithfield, EC1
Underground: Barbican (*not Suns.*)
St. Paul's
Bus: 4, 8, 22, 25, 141, 277, 279, 279A,
501, 502

St. Clement Danes Church
Strand, WC2
Underground: Temple (*not Suns.*)
Bus: see Roman Bath

St. Dunstan-in-the-West Church
Fleet Street, EC4
Underground: Temple (*not Suns.*)
Bus: 4, 6, 9, 11, 15, 171, 502, 513

St. George's Church
Hanover Square, W1
Underground: Oxford Circus
Bus: 3, 6, 12, 13, 15, 25, 53, 88, 159

St. James's Park, SW1
Underground: St. James's Park,
Trafalgar Square, Green Park
Bus: see *Houses of Parliament* and 9, 14,
19, 22, 25, 38 to St. James's Street

St. James's Square, SW1   see *Albany*

St. John's Church, Smith Square, SW1
see *Houses of Parliament*

St. Martin-in-the-Fields Church
Trafalgar Square, WC2
Underground: Charing Cross
Bus: see *Duke of York's Column*

St. Marylebone Parish Church
Marylebone Road
Underground: Baker Street
Bus: 1, 2, 2B, 13, 18, 18A, 27, 30, 74, 113, 159, 176

St. Mary-le-Bow Church
Underground: Bank, Mansion House
Bus: 6, 8, 9, 11, 15, 21, 22, 23, 25, 43, 76, 133, 501, 502, 513

St. Mary-le-Strand Church
Strand, EC2
Underground: Temple (*not Suns.*)
Bus: see *Roman Bath*

St. Paul's Cathedral
St. Paul's Churchyard, EC4
CATHEDRAL Daily from 0800 to 1900
(1800 Suns.)
(Oct. to Mar. closes at 1700)
CRYPT, GALLERIES Mons., Weds., Fris.
1000 to 1700 (1600 in winter). Tues.,
Thurs., Sats., Saints Days 1100 to 1700
(1600 in winter). Last tickets 40 mins.
before close.
Times subject to alteration for special
services
Admission Crypt 40p, children 20p;
Galleries 60p, children 25p
Underground: St. Paul's,
Mansion House
Bus: 4, 6, 8, 9, 11, 15, 18, 22, 25, 76, 141, 501, 502, 513

Smithfield Market
Charterhouse Street, EC1
Underground: Farringdon,
Barbican (*not Suns.*)
Bus: 4, 5, 8, 18, 22, 25, 45, 46, 55, 63, 168A, 221, 243, 259, 277, 279, 279A

Somerset House, Strand, WC2
Mons. to Fris. from 1000 to 1630,
Closed New Year's Day, Good Fri.,
Easter Mon. and Tues., 5 May, Spring
and Late Summer Hol. Mons.,
Christmas Eve and Day, Boxing Day,
27 and 28 Dec.
Underground: Temple (*not Suns.*)
Bus: 1, 4, 6, 9, 11, 13, 15, 55, 68, 77, 77A, 77C, 168, 170, 171, 172, 176, 188, 239, 502, 513

Spitalfields Market
Commercial Street, E1

Underground: Liverpool Street
Bus: 5, 6, 8, 8A, 22, 22A, 35, 47, 48, 67, 78, 149

Staple Inn, Holborn, WC1
Underground: Chancery Lane
(*not Suns.*)
Bus: 8, 18, 22, 25, 45, 171, 243, 259, 501

Stock Exchange
Throgmorton Street, EC2
Visitors' Gallery: Mons. to Fris.
from 0945 to 1530
Closed New Year's Day, Good Fri.,
Easter Mon., 5 May, Spring and Late
Summer Hol. Mons., Christmas Eve
and Day, Boxing Day. Free
see *Bank of England*

Temple (Middle and Inner)
Middle Temple Lane, EC4
MIDDLE TEMPLE HALL. Sat. 1000 to
1600. Usually also Mon. to Fri. 1000 to
1200 and 1500 to 1630
Closed New Year's Day, Easter Mon.,
5 May, Spring and Late Summer Hol.
Mons., Christmas Day, Boxing Day
TEMPLE CHURCH. Daily 1000 to 1700
(winter, closes at 1630)
Closed Christmas Day except for
services and Boxing Day
Underground: Temple (*not Suns.*)
Bus: 4, 6, 9, 11, 15, 171, 502, 513

Temple Bar, Theobald's Park,
Cheshunt, Herts.
British Rail: Theobald's Grove
Bus: 242, 283 to Theobald's Lane
then 1 mile walk

Tower of London
Tower Hill, EC3
Mar. to Oct. Mons. to Sats. 0930 to
1700, Suns. 1400 to 1700. Nov. to Feb.
Mons. to Sats. 0930 to 1600.
£1.50 (£1.00 Mar. to June and Sept. to
Oct., 50p Nov. and Dec.) Children and
pensioners 50p (30p Nov. and Dec.).
(all charges under review)
JEWEL HOUSE 50p, children 20p
Unaccompanied children under
10 not admitted
Closed New Year's Day, Good Fri.,
Christmas Eve and Day, Boxing Day
Underground: Tower Hill
Bus: 9, 42, 78